New Kids on the Net

Internet NetWork for Young Learners

New Kids on the Net

Internet NetWork
for Young Learners

Sheryl Burgstahler
University of Washington

Illustrated by Travis Burgstahler

Allyn and Bacon
Boston London Toronto
Sydney Tokyo Singapore
http://www.abacon.com/

Between the time Website information is gathered and then published, it is not unusual for some sites to have closed. Also, the transcription of URLs can result in unintended typographical errors. The publisher would appreciate notification where these occur so that they may be corrected in subsequent editions. Thank you.

Many of the designations used by manufacturers and sellers to distinguish their products are claimed as trademarks. Where those designations appear in this book, and Allyn & Bacon was aware of a trademark claim, the designations are marked with a ™ or ®.

Copyright © 1998 by Allyn & Bacon
A Viacom Company
160 Gould Street
Needham Heights, MA 02194

Internet: www.abacon.com
America Online: keyword: College Online

Permissions/Trademarks/Copyrights begin on page 189 which constitutes an extension of the copyright page.

ISBN 0-205-27698-9

Printed in the United States of America

10 9 8 7 6 5 4 3 2 1   01 00 99 98 97

Acknowledgments

Special thanks to the illustrator and "co-author" of this book, my son Travis. He helped choose the NetWork and tested the activities during his kindergarten year. We surfed the Net side-by-side and learned that sometimes we have different ideas about what's "boring," what's "cool," and what's "really cool." When in doubt, I trusted his judgment about whether a particular resource should be included in the book.

This book is dedicated to my mother.
She taught me what it means
to learn new things side-by-side.
When I was young there wasn't an Internet,
but I have no doubt that if there were we
would have explored it – together, side-by-side.

Contents

Contents .... **vii**

Preface .... **xi**
    About this Book xii
    Internet and Young Learners xiii
    Teaching and Learning xvi
    What You Will Need xvii
    Writing Conventions xviii

Chapter One 1
NetWork for Teachers and Parents **1**
    Notes to Teachers and Parents 1
    NetWork: Internet Basics 3
    NetWork: E-mail Basics 5

NetWork: Distribution List Basics 7
NetWork: WWW Basics 9
NetWork: Explore WWW Sites for Parents and Teachers 11
NetWork: Other Internet Tools 13
NetWork: Search the Internet 15
NetWork: Internet Safety 17

Chapter Two 19
NetWork for Young Learners: Language Arts, Social Studies 19
Notes to Teachers and Parents 19
NetWork: Join Katie in her Quest 21
NetWork: Tots TV, Lamb Chops and More! 23
NetWork: Webster the Spider 25
NetWork: Where's Arthur? 27
NetWork: Tell a Wacky Web Tale 29
NetWork: Visit Mr. Rogers' Neighborhood 31
NetWork: Alex's Scribbles 33
NetWork: Storybooks Online 35
NetWork: Moo in MooTown 37
NetWork: Join Alice in Internetland 39
NetWork: Visit Seussville 41
NetWork: The Brave and Bold Squirrel 43
NetWork: Candlelight Stories 45
NetWork: Meet My Hero 47
NetWork: Send an Internet Greeting Card 49
NetWork: McGuffie Avenue Gang 51
NetWork: Kody's Beary Scary Story 53
NetWork: Safety First! 55
NetWork: Meet Theodore Tugboat 57
NetWork: Get Caught in a Kids' Net 59
NetWork: Visit the Platypus Family Playroom 61
NetWork: International Kids' Space 63
NetWork: Ride the Bus with Curious George 65
NetWork: The Prince and I 67
NetWork: Publish or Perish 69
NetWork: Stop for Tea with Hello Kitty 71
NetWork: Welcome to the White House 73
NetWork: Story Time 75

Chapter Three 77
NetWork for Young Learners: Science, Mathematics 77
Notes to Teachers and Parents 77
NetWork: Under the Sea 79
NetWork: Soar with the Airplanes 81
NetWork: Mr. Flibby 83

NetWork: Bean Time 85
NetWork: Hop on the Magic School Bus 87
NetWork: Space Coloring Book 89
NetWork: Beautiful Butterflies 91
NetWork: KidsXone 93
NetWork: Animals in Australia 95
NetWork: Find Your Rainbow 97
NetWork: Build a Monster 99
NetWork: Join Billy Bear in the Playground 101
NetWork: Dream about the Dinosaurs 103
NetWork: Jump Start Elementary 105
NetWork: Zoom to the Zoo 107
NetWork: Recycle 109
NetWork: Stroll Down Sesame Street 111
NetWork: Mr. Edible Starchy Tuber Head 113
NetWork: Crayola 115
NetWork: Tackle Tic Tac Toe 117
NetWork: Visit Coco and Loco 119
NetWork: Endangered Species 121
NetWork: This is for the Birds! 123
NetWork: Interactive Fun 125
NetWork: Breakfast on the Web 127

Chapter Four 129
NetWork for Young Learners: Arts, Crafts, Entertainment **129**
Notes to Teachers and Parents 129
NetWork: Web-a-Sketch 131
NetWork: Wish with Wishupons 133
NetWork: Enter an Art Contest 135
NetWork: Color with Carlos 137
NetWork: Go On-line with Orbill 139
NetWork: Color with Kendra 141
NetWork: Disney On-line 143
NetWork: MCA's Coloring Corner 145
NetWork: Dalmations, Pinocchio, Beauty, Beast, and More! 147
NetWork: Join the ACEKids 149
NetWork: Toys, Toys, and More Toys! 151
NetWork: Crafts for Fun 153

Chapter Five 155
NetWork for Young Learners: More to Explore **155**
Notes to Teachers and Parents 155
NetWork: Become a Web Explorer 157
NetWork: Surf Web Collections 159
NetWork: Search WWW 161

Chapter Six 163
Find More Stuff: On-line Internet Guides and Directories 163
    Notes to Teachers and Parents 163
    Guides and Directories 164

Chapter Seven 169
Create More Lessons 169
    Notes to Teachers and Parents 169
    Lesson Template 171

In Plain English: A Glossary 173

Index 183

Preface

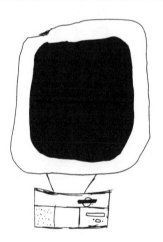

Are you a parent, teacher, child care worker, or computer lab assistant who would like to guide young children through meaningful experiences on the Internet, but

1) you doubt there is material appropriate for non-readers?

2) you don't know where to find resources for kids?

3) you don't have time to surf the Net to find materials?

4) you think URL might stand for Underground Rude Lizards, some impolite new cartoon characters trying to take over the sewers of the Teenage Mutant Ninja Turtles®?

If you answered "yes" to question number four, you need to do a little homework before jumping into these activities with your child. I suggest you work through the companion book *New Kids on the Net: A Tutorial for Teachers, Parents, and Students* first. The tutorial gives step-by-step instructions for getting started with Internet tools. You can also find many other Internet books in your local book store or library.

If you answered "no" to number four, but "yes" to at least one of the other three questions, this book is for you. Research and preparation take time and time is what you don't have enough of! *New Kids on the Net: Internet NetWork for Young Learners* saves your time by providing ready-to-use materials to help young children get started on exciting adventures on the Internet.

About this Book

Chapter One: NetWork for Teachers and Parents includes NetWork to help you review Internet skills and find resources before you engage in Internet activities with young learners. In addition, in *Chapter Six* you will find lists of electronic books, tutorials, and other reference materials available over the Internet. Throughout the book, technical words are explained using non-technical terms. A glossary (in plain English) is provided as an appendix.

The *Chapter One* introduction is followed by four chapters that are bursting with activities to engage young children, particularly preschoolers through first graders. They cover the content areas of language arts, social studies, science, mathematics, arts, crafts, and entertainment. In all cases, emphasis is placed on development of beginning reading and writing skills. Each *NetWork for Young Learners* chapter begins with a section titled *Notes to Teachers and Parents* that outlines the prerequisites, objectives, student activities, and references for the chapter. The chapter introduction is followed by a set of NetWork worksheets; each one includes both on-line (using the computer) and off-line (not using the computer) activities.

Engage in NetWork activities with individual students, small groups, or an entire class. Use them in day care, traditional school, home school, after school, and summer camp settings. Distribute NetWork activities in pre-service and in-service courses for educators who work with young children and let them play the role of a young learner.

Choose from more than sixty two-page, tear-out activity sheets. They are easy to find; each title is preceded by the graphic

⬛➤ NetWork:

Pick the lessons and the order most appropriate for your children. Pull out your favorite activity sheets and organize them in your own notebooks or files. Integrate them with the curriculum of your day care or school. Whether you're using the NetWork in a school or at home, consider setting up a schedule for completing the NetWork activity sheets – how about one each week? Even very young children will enjoy putting their names on completed worksheets. So, be ready with gold stars and make room on a refrigerator or bulletin board to display completed off-line NetWork.

Many of the Internet resources selected for NetWork include a rich set of links to other resources for activity extensions and new activities; a template for creating your own activity sheets is included in *Chapter Seven*. Although most of the NetWork activities in this book involve paper-and-pencil tasks, be creative as children are motivated by the Internet gems they find. Create a play, go on a nature walk, take a field trip to the zoo, interview a friend, collect seeds in your kitchen, grow a plant, decorate a cake – you are limited only by the collective imaginations of you and your young learners.

I have to be honest with you and warn you that any printed publication about the Internet, including this book, starts to become outdated the moment it is written. Even though I updated addresses and instructions right up to the publication deadline, the Internet world is dynamic. Every day people are adding, updating, and discontinuing services. Do not be surprised if you find that resources described in the lessons here or in other reference materials operate differently than described or no longer exist at all! Further, there may be differences in screen displays when resources are accessed using different types of computers and software programs. Consequently, what these materials describe may not always be exactly what you see on your screen. On the bright side, I selected resources for this book that are likely to be supported in the future and to expand as the Internet does. There is a good chance that by the time you access them, they will have content and features beyond those noted in this book. The Internet is getting better and better.

Internet and Young Learners

In his *Call to Action for American Education in the 21st Century*, President Clinton stated that to prepare America for the 21st century, we need to have strong, safe schools with clear standards of achievement; challenge parents to get involved early in their children's learning; connect every classroom and library to the Internet; and help all students become technologically literate. However, the Internet was not designed for young learners. It was originally used only by researchers. Slowly, information for the rest of us has appeared on the Internet – lately, at an explosive rate. More and more materials are now available for the younger set.

With my son Travis in kindergarten, I became interested in whether there might be some Internet resources that he and I could enjoy together. I hoped to find activities that are interactive, educational, open-ended, and fun for Travis. I especially hoped to find engaging Internet sites where he would return again and again. What I found was both encouraging and discouraging. First, the bad news:

- Many sites related to children's topics are commercial and are devoted more to selling products than to entertaining or educating children. Travis often wants to search for information about toys he sees in commercials on television – now we have a tool for immediately finding out where the newest toys can be purchased and at what price (a dream come true for us parents, right?).

- Many sites are composed primarily of text; they require a lot of reading and are more suitable for older learners.

- Sites often employ graphics that take a long time to arrive on your computer screen – this is a problem for me, but more of a problem for the little person at my side whose attention span is even shorter than mine.

- Not many resources are interactive yet and you sometimes need special software to use audio, video, and other special features.

- It takes a lot of time to find resources of interest to you and your child. And, many are only fun once; they are not engaging enough to motivate a return visit.

Now, the good news:

- We found many engaging activities. Some encouraged Travis to read and write; some motivated him to create related non-computer activities. For example, when he worked through a Muppet Treasure Island activity, we ended up spending a whole evening setting up a treasure hunt in our house. Travis developed the clues, I helped him write them on slips of paper, and we hid them together. We had a great time, and dad enjoyed participating in the hunt, too. I didn't bother telling Travis that he was practicing his writing, spelling, cutting, and problem-solving skills.

- Some Internet sites maintain collections of links to other sites with related materials. So, once we got started with a few interesting resources, we immediately had access to many more.

- The number of entertaining and educational resources for young learners is growing each day.

- You do not have to worry about searching for updates; when you access a resource you always reach the latest version.

- Travis is Internet literate. He knows what the Net is. He automatically says stuff like "maybe we can find it on the Internet" when he needs some information. He knows that you need an address to go somewhere on the Internet. He knows how to point and click, scroll, and pull down menus. He knows that you can search for things of interest to you and that sometimes you don't immediately find what you are looking for so you search some more, using different words. He knows that the Internet is a source of information and fun – simply a part of his world like books, newspapers, televisions, telephones, and radios.

So, after my explorations with Travis, would I recommend that parents of a preschooler rush out and purchase a computer system and Internet account for their child? Probably not. But, many families already have a computer and Internet connection or plan to get one for other purposes. If this is the case, you can use this book to help your youngster join in the fun on the Net. Preschool and kindergarten teachers likewise can use these activities for the periodic classroom trips to school computer labs.

When working with children who do not yet read or write or are in the early stages of developing these skills, you will need to work side-by-side with one young learner or a group of children. Read the instructions and content aloud, but be sure to encourage their involvement. Follow the steps for completing on- and off-line activities together. When writing is required, act as scribe, but let children compose the creations. With Travis, he quickly learned to type his name on the keyboard. As we participated in writing activities, he typed some words with my coaching and, at other times, he dictated the words for me to enter. Similarly, in the off-line NetWork activities he dictated to me (his scribe) or he wrote words and sentences with my help. In each case he was developing writing skills. The Internet activities motivated him to do so.

Teaching and Learning

The Internet opens doors to collaborative learning between children and adults. This can be an exciting step away from the old-style approach where the adult simply delivers information to the child. Instead, parents, teachers, and children can explore and learn side-by-side. Exploratory learning allows teachers and parents to serve as facilitators, coaches, and guides rather than as sources of knowledge and dispensers of information. A facilitator of learning helps students gain skills in research, critical thinking, and problem solving that are valuable while pursuing academic studies and other life experiences. Most adults find it's fun to be the "guide on the side" instead of the "sage on the stage." Adults and children can even alternate in the roles of guide and learner as they explore resources together. This relationship results in child-centered learning rather than the traditional teacher- or parent-centered learning.

While working with children on Internet activities, it is important to adjust to different learning styles and skill levels. There is also a wide range of levels of enthusiasm when it comes to learning with technology – don't assume that all children love to use computers. When guiding the activities of children, pose questions which address different levels of intellectual behavior. Some examples follow.

knowledge: Name the President of the United States.

comprehension: Tell me what the story was about.

application: Explain how you could help recycle cans at your home.

analysis: Describe what the children could have done differently so they would not have gotten lost in the woods.

synthesis: Name the most important things you need to take when you go camping.

evaluation: Tell Arthur™ what you like best about his stories.

If you're a professional educator, you may recognize these levels as part of Bloom's Taxonomy.

Finally, don't forget the affective domain, that is, how children feel about the experiences they have on the Internet. It is important that children learn to develop and express their attitudes, concerns, and responsibilities – you'll find many opportunities to work in the affective domain while exploring Internet resources. Encourage children to express their opinions and feelings about the resources they find. For example, early on in our Internet adventures, Travis became frustrated because he had to wait so long for his Internet finds to appear on the screen. After expressing his frustration with great emotion, he came up with his own solution to the problem – he now brings a coloring book along so he has something to do while he waits.

The NetWork worksheets in this publication apply these concepts; consider them as you develop your own worksheets and other educational activities.

What You Will Need

The most important prerequisites for learning about the Internet are a healthy curiosity about this technology, an eagerness to develop new skills and applications, a basic understanding of computer use (e.g., how to use a computer for word processing or other applications), patience, and the adventuresome spirit of a pioneer. You will also find that developing Internet skills and exploring Internet resources require a significant investment in time.

NetWork activities are designed for hands-on learning. To complete the exercises, you need a personal computer that has access to the Internet. There are many options for obtaining an Internet account. You may have access through your school or through a private Internet service provider. It does not matter what kind of computer you use, but software and hardware (e.g., a modem) which can connect to the Internet are required. The Internet tools (software) that you have access to depend upon the capabilities of your computer as well as your access mode. To take full advantage of the activities presented, you will need a modem with a speed of 14.4 or higher (the faster the better) and graphically-based World Wide Web browser software (e.g., Netscape Navigator™, Microsoft Internet Explorer ™). A color monitor is not absolutely required, but provides a real advantage when working with young children.

If you are working with a child who has a disability, explore hardware and software options that will provide as much independence as possible in operating the computer and accessing Internet resources. For example, screen reading software coupled with a speech synthesizer allows a child who is blind to hear spoken words whenever text appears on the screen. Special input devices allow a child with limited hand function to operate a computer.

Writing Conventions

Computer interactions are difficult to describe in writing. In order to help you interpret the material in this book, the following conventions have been adopted. Review them quickly now and refer back to this section later if necessary, but don't worry about memorizing them. In most cases, you will find their meaning is self-evident when you see the context in which they are used.

- Names of special keys are enclosed in pointed brackets. For example, a direction to press the key on your keyboard labeled "tab" might be written

  press \<tab>

- On your keyboard the key which moves you to the start of the next line may be labeled "enter," "return" or some other term. In these materials, this key is represented by

  \<return>

- The key to move left and delete a character may be labeled "backspace," or "delete" on your keyboard. In these materials, this key is represented by

  \<backspace>

- Some actions require that you hold down the control key while you push another key. These commands are represented with the ^ (caret) preceding the key. For example, the direction to press the \<ctrl> key and the "x" key at the same time could be written

  press ^x

- Information that the computer displays on a screen, computer host names, and Internet addresses are shown in `courier` non-proportional typeface. Courier™ is a familiar typewriter typeface that looks like this:

  `folder to save message in (saved messages):`

- Some information you will type in exactly as shown and some information you will substitute the appropriate information for the specific case (e.g., your personal name).

Information that you type exactly as shown is presented in **`boldface courier`**. For example, if you are expected to type the word "anonymous" the instruction would be presented as

type **`anonymous`**

Information that you provide appears in ***`boldface italics courier`***. For example, if you are to type your own first name and then your last name, the instructions may read

type ***`Firstname Lastname`***

- Computer systems which you will encounter on the Internet are often case-sensitive. This means that it makes a difference if you type **Q** or **q**. When lesson instructions call for lowercase letters, be sure to type in lowercase letters and when instructions call for uppercase, type in uppercase.

See you on the Net!

Sheryl Burgstahler, Ph. D.

Allyn and Bacon WWW home page:
`http://www.abacon.com/`

Chapter One
NetWork for Teachers and Parents

Notes to Teachers and Parents

You're anxious to jump in and explore resources with your young learner. But, first, it is important to brush up on your own skills. This chapter gives you an opportunity to do that and to find useful resources along the way.

Prerequisites

In order to complete the NetWork in this chapter you will need access to a computer, the Internet network, and World Wide Web browser software.

Objectives

This chapter is for you, the teacher or parent, to develop or review basic Internet skills. By the end of this chapter you will:

- understand the functions of basic Internet tools;

- be able to access resources using electronic mail, distribution lists, and the World Wide Web;

- be able to find resources to support parents and teachers helping children learn, both on and off the Internet;

- know where to find resources to develop new Internet skills; and

- understand how to keep children safe on the Internet.

Activities

1. Complete the NetWork in this chapter to review Internet skills and locate useful resources.

2. Review *In Plain English: A Glossary*, which provides descriptions of terms commonly encountered when using the Internet.

References

Chapter Six lists on-line resources for further exploration of the Internet.

NetWork: Internet Basics

Overview

"Networking" can refer to people talking to people (to be successful in business these days, you need to "network" with the right people) or to computers communicating with computers (possibly to share printers, files or electronic mail). Well, guess what? The Internet network, also called the Net, connects computers so that people can network!

So where did the Internet come from? A predecessor of the Internet network is ARPANet. ARPA stands for Advanced Research Projects Administration, a branch of the Department of Defense. ARPANet was created in the late 1960's to link military research contractors, including many universities. ARPANet became difficult to manage as the number of users grew and was eventually divided into two networks. Internet Protocol (IP) was developed to enable the traffic of one network to travel to the other and was designed to allow thousands of other networks to do the same. Later, the National Science Foundation set up five supercomputer centers for use by researchers from all over the country. It incorporated IP in building the NSFNET network to accomplish this. The slower ARPANet eventually shut down. By the mid-1990's several large commercial Internet networks had emerged.

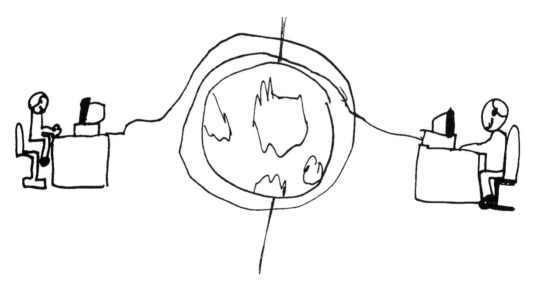

So, the Internet is a network of networks that all communicate with each other thanks to the Internet Protocol. One important characteristic of a network is its size. You can access more people and more resources on the Internet than on any other network in the world. The Internet connects your computer to thousands of computers around the world. They are connected by wiring them together, over phone lines, and via satellite transmissions. Networks that are part of the Internet include large corporate networks like Microsoft, IBM and Boeing Company; universities and community colleges; K-12 schools; small businesses; non-profit organizations; government agencies; and Internet service providers. People make information available on the Internet; if they are willing to share, you can use it. A vast collection of information is free to Internet users.

For many people the Internet will be a key to making lifelong learning a reality. You can enroll in college classes taught over the Internet by instructors who live thousands of miles away and whose students come from all over the world. With the Internet you can go on field trips far beyond the reach of your family van or school bus.

Internet Tools

Once connected to the Internet, you can access millions of people and thousands of information resources by using basic Internet tools. Below is a summary of some of the things you can do on the Internet matched with the electronic tools available to perform these functions.

Functions	Tools
Communicate one-to-one or in small groups.	Electronic mail
Discussion in groups	Distribution lists Usenet newsgroups
General-purpose interfaces to resources	Gopher World Wide Web (WWW)
Log on to other computers	Telnet
Transfer files between computers	File transfer protocol (FTP)

Things to Think About

1. What information would you like to access over the Internet?

2. What Internet tools are you most likely to use to access these resources?

NetWork: E-mail Basics

Overview

Electronic mail (e-mail) is similar to postal mail (often called "snail mail" by e-mail users) and telephone conversations except that e-mail messages are composed on computers and transmitted over electronic networks. Many e-mail software programs (e.g., Eudora™, PINE™) are provided by or recommended by your host organization or Internet service provider. You can use e-mail to communicate with people world-wide. For example, you could communicate with a friend in England, students in a classroom in Brazil, or even the president of the United States. You can choose people to communicate with based on common interests, unconstrained by physical locations and schedules. E-mail enables you to:

- send messages addressed to specific people;

- receive messages from others;

- send messages to and receive messages from members of a group; and

- request and receive information.

E-mail has advantages over telephone communication and postal mail. It's much faster than postal mail – your message is usually delivered within minutes. It's more convenient than the telephone because receivers do not need to be at their computers at the time your messages are sent; their host computers store the messages until they are ready to read them. Another advantage of e-mail is that you can quickly reach groups of people by addressing a single message to a group name. With these powerful features, it is no wonder e-mail is the most popular tool on the Internet.

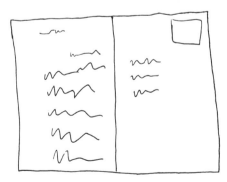

One word of caution is in order. E-mail should not be considered private. Electronic mail is more like a postcard than a letter sealed in an envelope. It is more like a phone conversation on a party line than one on a private line. Consequently, it is not an appropriate method for delivering messages which must be kept private.

Activities

1. Do you need something to brighten your day or lighten your load? Send e-mail to

    almanac@oes.orst.edu

    Leave the subject line blank. For the text of the message, type

    send moral-support

    Soon you should receive a message from Almanac via electronic mail.

    To receive a guide to the almanac resource, which is maintained by the Oregon Extension Service, send a message to the same address with **send guide** as the message. The guide will give you information about how to use this resource.

2. AskERIC is a service for K-12 teachers, library media specialists, and administrators. Using the extensive resources of the ERIC system, AskERIC staff answer your questions about curriculum, learning, teaching, information technology, and administration. Send a question to

    askERIC@ericir.syr.edu

    Expect a response within 48 hours.

3. Roadmap is an on-line tutorial about the Internet written by Patrick Crispen at the University of Alabama. To get information about how to obtain the lessons, address an e-mail message to

    listserv@ua1vm.ua.edu

    Leave the subject line blank. In the body of your message type

    get map package F=MAIL

NetWork: Distribution List Basics

Overview and Procedures

Distribution lists create communities of people with shared interests. List management software programs reside on many computers throughout the Internet, managing thousands of distribution lists. Common names of list managers include LISTSERV, ListProcessor™, and Majordomo. Each computer that has list management software maintains subscriptions to one or more distribution lists. To subscribe to and unsubscribe from a list you communicate with the list management software. To communicate with the members of a list you send electronic mail to the distribution list address.

Subscribe

To subscribe to a LISTSERV or ListProc distribution list, send a message to the list manager address. Leave the `Subject:` line blank and type in the body of the message

> **`subscribe`** *`listname`* ***`Firstname Lastname`***

where ***`listname`*** is the name of the list and ***`Firstname Lastname`*** means to type in your full name. To subscribe to a Majordomo list, type your full e-mail address in place of ***`Firstname Lastname`***.

You will get a message back to confirm that you have been added to the list or provide further instructions for joining the list. You may also receive other useful information about the list.

Lurk, Reply, Post

Shortly after you subscribe to a distribution list that is for discussion you will begin receiving messages from members of the list. Begin participation by just reading messages. Some call this "lurking." Do not feel compelled to post questions or comments during your first days as a subscriber. By spending some time lurking in a new group, you can learn about the group's interests and culture. Before posting a question or comment to a list, make certain that the issue you are raising is appropriate, given the topic of the list and the culture established by its members.

Use the reply command in your electronic mail software to reply to a message that has been posted to the list. Check carefully that your reply is set up as you intend. If you want to reply to the whole group, the address should be the distribution list address. If you want to reply to just the person posting the message and not the whole group, make sure that only the individual's e-mail address is included in the `To:` line.

Post a message by sending e-mail to the distribution list address. The list manager software distributes your message to everyone on the list.

Unsubscribe

If you want to cancel your subscription to a distribution list, send a message to the list manager with the message

unsubscribe *listname*

where **listname** is the name of the distribution list. Another command commonly used to unsubscribe from a list is `Signoff`.

Get Help

To get a list of functions and commands to use in corresponding with the list manager software, send a message to the list manager with the message

help

You will soon receive a helpful message from the list manager software.

Activities

Practice your skills by subscribing to at least one of the following distribution lists:

List Name	List Manager Address	Topic
aparent	listserv@sjuvm.stjohns.edu	adoptive parents
biling-fam	majordomo@nvg.unit.no	bilingual families
easi	listserv@sjuvm.stjohns.edu	adaptive technology
ecenet-l	listserv@vmd.cso.uiuc.edu	early childhood education
ednet	listproc@lists.umass.edu	K-12 education
home-ed	majordomo@world.std.com	home schooling
kidsphere	kidsphere-request@vms.cis.pitt.edu	KIDSPHERE
our-kids	listserv@maelstrom.stjohns.edu	special needs kids
parenting-l	listserv@postoffice.cso.uiuc.edu	parenting
preemie-l	majordomo@vicnet.net.au	premature babies
shp-list	majordomo@lists.sonic.net	stay-at-home parenting
tagfam	listserv@sjuvm.stjohns.edu	families of gifted kids
tesl-l	listserv@cunyvm.cuny.edu	ESL teachers
w2moms	majordomo@pobox.com	working moms

 **NetWork: WWW Basics**

Overview

The World Wide Web is the latest and greatest tool on the Internet. Affectionately called the Web, WWW or W3, this tool makes all Internet resources available through a single easy-to-use interface. It was developed in Switzerland at CERN (Conseil European pour la Recherche Nucleaire), the European Laboratory for Particle Physics. In the Web, you begin at an opening screen (or several screens) called a "home page." The home page generally provides an outline of resources you will find at the site. It also provides a gateway to other related Internet resources; some are local to the server, many are miles away on other computer systems on the Internet.

WWW allows you to connect to a wide variety of types of resources. It uses the concept of "hypertext." A word or phrase (or area of a page) is linked to other words (or files or directories) or to other resources on the Internet. A hypertext link is usually represented by an icon or a series of words that are underlined. When you select a hypertext link, you connect to a new page or another Internet resource. The Web incorporates other Internet tools such as Gopher, Telnet, and file transfer protocol (FTP), making it possible to access resources available with these tools through one easy-to-use interface.

To access the World Wide Web, you use client software called a browser. Client software running on your system transfers information to and from other servers on the network. When you click to activate a WWW link, your Web browser invokes a series of commands to retrieve information from a remote computer. Sophisticated graphical browsers allow you to work with WWW's multimedia capabilities and are installed on your personal computer. Text-based browsers display only the text and are installed on Internet host computers.

URL Basics

When you use WWW, each pointer to a resource is written in a logical and precise format called a Uniform Resource Locator (URL). A URL is like a bibliographic citation, but, instead of telling you how to find a printed publication, a URL tells you (and your browser software) how to find an Internet resource. Although I am going to explain more about URLs, don't be intimidated – once you get going, you'll find that there isn't really much you need to remember about these.

A URL typically contains the following information: a protocol (i.e., a system or procedure that computers agree upon for making the link), an Internet address, a directory path, and a file name. For example, consider the following URL which points to a resource on the Internet:

```
http://wings.buffalo.edu/world/vt2
```

The parts of this URL consist of a protocol (`http://`), an Internet address (`wings.buffalo.edu`), separator `/`, a directory path (`world`), another separator `/`, and a file name (`vt2`). An optional `/` may appear at the end. This example demonstrates the basic form of a URL, but you will run into examples where there are many more sections after the protocol.

The protocol for making a link is related to the Internet tool accessed with the link. In a URL, the abbreviation for the resource type is followed by `://`. HyperText Transfer Protocol (HTTP) is the method that WWW sites use to communicate with each other. Below is a list of the beginning characters of URLs for popular Internet tools.

URL Beginning	Tool
`mailto://`	electronic mail
`http://`	WWW
`gopher://`	Gopher
`telnet://`	Telnet
`ftp://`	file transfer protocol
`news://`	Usenet Newsgroups

Things to Think About

1. How do you access the Internet (e.g., through a school or private account with an Internet service provider)?

2. What browser software do you use? How do you activate it?

3. How much WWW technical information should you present to the children you work with? How can you present it to young learners so that they will understand the basic concepts?

 ## NetWork: Explore WWW Sites for Parents and Teachers

Overview

Whether you're home schooling your children, teaching preschool or kindergarten, or just looking for a rainy day activity, look to the Web to gain insights into working with young learners, find curricular ideas, and locate resources.

Procedure

To find resources for parents and teachers, access the URLs

Bess, the Internet Retriever™
http://www.bess.net

Classroom Connect
http://www.classroom.net

Clearinghouse on Elementary and Early Childhood Education
http://ericps.ed.uiuc.edu/

Closing the Gap
http://www.closingthegap.com/

The CyberMom™ Dot Com
http://www.thecybermom.com/

Early Childhood Education & Activity Resources
**http://www.intex.net/~dlester/pam/preschool/
    preschoolpage.html**

Educational Software Institute
http://www.edsoft.com/q/index.html

FACES of Adoption
http://nac.adopt.org/adopt/

Family Planet
http://family.starwave.com/index.html

Family Surfboard™ Parents' Electronic Resource Center
http://www.familysurf.com/resource.htm

Family.com
http://www.family.com

Global SchoolNet Foundation
http://www.gsn.org

HotList of K-12 Internet School Sites
http://rrnet.com/~gleason/k12.html

Instructional Television
http://www.pbs.org/itv/

KidSource OnLine ™
http://www.kidsource.com/

Learning Train
http://www.macconnect.com/~jrpotter/ltrain.spml

National Center for Missing and Exploited Children
http://www.missingkids.org/

Resources for Families of Missing Children
http://www.att.com/tobesafe/

Parent Soup™
http://www.parentsoup.com/

ParentsPlace.com™
http://www.parentsplace.com/

Summer Fun
http://www.ok.bc.ca/TEN/summer/mainpage.html

Teachers Helping Teachers
http://pacificnet.net/~mandel/

Technology and Information Educational Services
http://www.ties.k12.mn.us/

U.S. Department of Education
http://www.ed.gov/

Web66: A K12 World Wide Web Project
http://web66.coled.umn.edu/

WWW4teachers
http://www.4teachers.org/home/

◗➤ NetWork: Other Internet Tools

Overview

In this chapter you have reviewed the use of electronic mail, distribution lists, and World Wide Web. What about the other Internet tools? I will not cover special procedures for using other tools directly because most of the resources of interest to young learners are accessible via the World Wide Web; in fact, you can use other Internet tools through your Web browser without even knowing that you are using them! If you would like to learn more about the tools briefly described below, refer to the on-line resources provided in *Chapter Six* or purchase a printed Internet reference book or user guide.

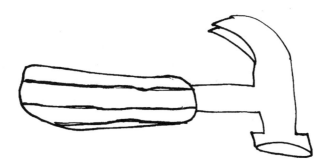

Gopher

Internet Gopher™ software was developed at the University of Minnesota and named after the University's mascot. It began as a campus-wide information server (CWIS) and evolved into a powerful interface to many Internet resources. It uses many levels of menus in a hierarchical structure, allowing you to search through well-organized collections of information and retrieve files for your local use. Many people predict that, since WWW has become so popular as an interface to Internet resources, Gopher may no longer play an important role on the Net. Maybe so, but there are still some Gopher servers in operation. You can access a Gopher server using special Gopher software. You can also access a Gopher server with a WWW browser; the URL begins with `gopher://`.

Telnet

Telnet is an Internet tool that allows you to connect to another computer. If you have an account on that computer or if the system allows access to guests, you can log on. You can use Telnet software directly or access Telnet sites with your World Wide Web browser. The URL of a Telnet site begins with `telnet://`.

FTP

The Internet contains many collections of files (archives) that are freely available to anyone who knows how to locate and retrieve them. FTP was once a common way for scientists to exchange scientific papers and data files. File transfer protocol (FTP) software allows you to transfer files from one computer to another. FTP files include software programs that run on your computer, text files (e.g., electronic journals, texts, newsletters, legal documents), graphics and image files, and collections of data. Besides using FTP directly, you can use World Wide Web and Gopher to access FTP sites. The URL of an FTP site begins with `ftp://`.

Usenet Newsgroups

Usenet is a collection of discussion forums (called newsgroups or discussion groups), each devoted to debate or discussion of a particular topic. People subscribe to a Usenet group because they are interested in the discussion group topic. There is a wide variety of topics – some serious, some light. With Usenet newsgroups, rather than messages coming into your e-mail mailbox as they do with distribution lists, you have to enter the Usenet bulletin board system to read them. This requires special newsreader software; you can also access newsgroups by using WWW browser software. When you join a Usenet group you can read the postings (messages) by other members of the group. You can reply to individuals in the discussion group or post your own for all members of the group to read. The URL of a newsgroup site begins with `news://`.

 # NetWork: Search the Internet

Overview

To find Internet resources of interest, you can surf the Net, following links that look promising; you can look through reference materials; and you can explore sites recommended by other people. You can also access Web sites that list other Internet resources; here are the URLs of several lists:

> The List Server Page
> **http://www.cuc.edu/cgi-bin/listservform.pl**
>
> Liszt, the mailing list directory
> **http://www.liszt.com/**
>
> Publicly Accessible Mailing Lists
> **http://www.neosoft.com/internet/paml/**
>
> Yanoff's Internet Services List
> **http://www.spectracom.com/islist/**

There are also search engines and other search tools that allow you to search the Web. Some are organized by topic. Some allow you to use keywords in your search; further, you can use the operators *and*, *or* and *not* with some search engines. For example, *tennis and children* would find resources that have to do with both tennis and children; whereas, *tennis or children* would find all resources related to either tennis or children – a very long list, I'm sure! Once a search engine identifies a resource of interest to you, click on the resource name and you will be linked to that site automatically. Below are URLs of some search tools on the Net.

> **http://altavista.digital.com/**
> **http://galaxy.einet.net/**
> **http://inktomi.berkeley.edu/**
> **http://lycos.cs.cmu.edu/**
> **http://metacrawler.cs.washington.edu/**
> **http://webcrawler.com/**
> **http://www.excite.com/**
> **http://www.four11.com/**
> **http://www.infoseek.com/**
> **http://www.mckinley.com/**
> **http://www.search.com**
> **http://www.yahoo.com/**

Procedure and Activities

Choose a topic that you would like to explore with young children. Look through resource lists. Then, use keywords with several search engines to obtain information about sites that deal with the topic. Compare the results.

URL Hint

If you try to access a resource using a URL and get an error message indicating that the site cannot be found, try typing the URL again; make sure that upper and lower cases are used correctly and that letter sequences are exactly right.

If you still get an error, try leaving off the last section (or more if necessary) to see if you can connect to the resource site. The reason this process works is that sometimes system administrators change the file names and the full URL will not work. But the site probably still exists, so you may be able to use the first part of the URL to enter the site and then look for the items of interest to you. For example, suppose you get an error message when you try to open

```
http://www.ab.cde/fg/hij/klmn/op.html
```

Next time try leaving off the end of the URL, for example try

```
http://www.ab.cde/fg/hij/klmn
```

If that doesn't work, shorten it further and try

```
http://www.ab.cde/fg/hij
```

The minimum you will need to access the WWW site includes the server's address (i.e., up to the first single /). In the example above, the minimum URL is

```
http://www.ab.cde
```

NetWork: Internet Safety

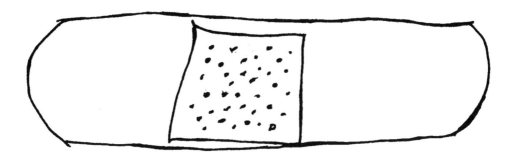

The Internet network creates unprecedented opportunities for meeting people and accessing resources. However, it was originally created for adult use. Although most people have positive experiences on the Net, there are cases where information access and electronic communications have resulted in exposure to offensive material and harassment. Children are particularly vulnerable to these risks.

Begin discussing household or classroom rules and safety guidelines at an early age. Below are examples of child safety guidelines for children using the Net.

- Never give out personal information (including street address, phone number, name of school) or send a picture to someone you have met on the network without the permission of your parents.

- Do not participate in conversations that would not be acceptable to your parents or teachers.

- Do not engage in conversations with which you are not comfortable. **Immediately report offensive or troubling electronic mail messages that you receive to a teacher or parent.**

- Never agree to get together in person with someone you "meet" on the Internet without the approval of your parents.

Adult supervision is the key to making sure that children access appropriate resources on the Internet. However, filter services and software programs are commercially available for helping parents and teachers control the resources to which children have access; they typically block access to sexually explicit Internet resources. If you are interested in exploring this option, consult a computer store or check out resources on the Internet to learn about options, effectiveness, and costs. Below are URLs of some Web sites that provide information about filtering software.

Bess, the Internet Retriever™, N2H2, Incorporated
`http://www.bess.net`

CyberPatrol®, Microsystems Software
`http://www.cyberpatrol.com`

Net Nanny™, Trove Investment Corporation
`http://web20.mindlink.net/netnanny`

SurfWatch™, Surf Watch Software, Inc.
`http://www.surfwatch.com`

Things to Think About

1. What are rules you can employ to help children stay safe on the Internet?

2. How might rules differ for children of different ages?

3. What are the respective roles of the school, parents, and the government in keeping children safe on the Internet?

4. What policies, rules, and procedures can be implemented at home and in the classroom to help keep children safe when using the Internet?

5. What actions should a school district take before providing children access to the Internet?

Chapter Two
NetWork for Young Learners:
Language Arts, Social Studies

I can read in red.
I can read in blue.
I can read in pickle color too.

– from *I Can Read with My Eyes Shut*, Dr. Seuss
http://www.randomhouse.com/seussville/games/whosaidthat.cgi

Notes to Teachers and Parents

Getting a good start in developing reading and writing skills is a high priority for all children. Your child will be developing language arts skills, whether you are reading to her or she is reading to you, whether she is writing or she is dictating a story to you, the scribe. Internet resources can provide early language arts and social studies activities as well as the motivation to develop basic skills. Reading and writing provide opportunities for quality adult-child interactions as well.

Prerequisites

In order to complete the NetWork in this chapter you will need access to a computer, the Internet network, and World Wide Web browser software.

Objectives

After completion of the NetWork in this chapter, young learners will be able to use the keyboard and mouse to perform basic functions on the computer and the World Wide Web. They will use Internet resources to develop basic reading, writing, and social studies skills. These activities will help young children learn to:

- choose stories to read;
- listen to stories read by others;
- recall details of a picture or story;
- draw an appropriate picture for a theme;
- dictate a story;
- recognize upper and lower case letters;
- identify letter sounds;
- read their own names;
- read words;
- read short sentences;
- write their names;
- write lower case and upper case letters;
- copy letters and words; and
- write their own addresses, birthdates, and phone numbers.

Student Activities

1. Review all materials in this chapter. Test activities. Edit and expand upon worksheets as appropriate for your children.

2. Choose appropriate NetWork worksheets; work through the exercises with the children, maximizing their participation. Read instructions to them or help them read. For writing exercises, children can do the writing or dictate to an adult, the scribe. Talk to them about their discoveries.

3. Extend the exercises and create more activities as appropriate.

References

Chapter Six lists on-line resources for further exploration of the Internet. *Chapter Seven* includes ideas for creating additional NetWork.

✏️ NetWork: Join Katie in her Quest

Overview

Katie's Quest is a story about a girl who has a great adventure in Lunaland. You can choose character names and print pictures to color.

Procedure

With your Web browser access the URL

http://africa.cis.co.za/kids/magz/kq/kq.html

Activities

1. Type names of people you know to make them part of the story. You'll need a:

   - girl's name
   - boy's name
   - pony's name

   Click a button to choose the color version or black and white version of the story. Print pages on your printer if you would like to color the pictures.

2. Click the **Online Books** icon to find more to explore.

3. Dictate or write a story about Katie and draw a picture to go with it.

Name_____

 ## NetWork: Tots TV, Lamb Chops and More!

Overview

Explore episodes and print pictures of Thomas the Tank Engine and his friends at Shining Time Station™. Meet the characters in Barney® & Friends, Lamb Chops™ Play-Along, Tots TV™, The Magic School Bus™, Mr. Rogers' Neighborhood™, Sesame Street™, Arthur™, Storytime™, and other PBS shows.

Procedure

With your Web browser access the URL

http://www.pbs.org/

Activities

1. Select **PBS Kids**. Select **Shining Time Station**. Browse through **EPISODE ACTIVITIES** to get some ideas of activities to complete. Select **ONLINE FUN FOR JUNIOR CONDUCTORS**. Select a picture to print and color. Here's one to try now.

Select **Shining Time Station Coloring Page Gallery** to see submissions from children. Return to the PBS Kids home page.

2. From the PBS Kids home page select **Tots TV**. Choose **English Version** or **Versión en español**. Select **Meet the Tots** to learn about Tiny, Tilly, and Tom. You'll even be able to see some puppet patterns. Here's one for Tiny that you can color.

Make puppets out of paper bags or cloth with a parent or teacher. Put on a puppet show. Your parent or teacher can check out the HOME section of the **Tots TV** home page to come up with more activities for you.

3. From the PBS Kids home page select **Arthur**, **Lamb Chops Play-Along**, **Mister Rogers' Neighborhood**, **Sesame Street**, **Storytime**, or other kids' shows. Read the stories and explore on-line activities.

Name_____

NetWork: Webster the Spider

Overview

Visit WebTime Stories™ with Webster the Spider. This is a great place for little Webcrawlers.

Procedure

With your Web browser access the URL

http://www.webtimestories.com/

Activities

1. Select **CHILDREN**. Select and read **Brandon's Cat**. Draw a picture of your pet or a pet that you would like to have.

2. Return to the **Children's Section**. Select and read **Mandy's Saturday**. Dictate or write a sentence and draw a picture about something you like to do on Saturday.

3. Read other selections at this site.

Name_____

✏️➤ NetWork: Where's Arthur?

Overview

Arthur™ is a popular television character with young learners. On the Arthur Web site fans can check out the schedule for telecasts and participate in activities.

Procedure

With your Web browser access the URL

http://www.pbs.org/wgbh/pages/arthur/

Activities

1. Arthur loves to read stories, hear stories read to him, and write stories. Select **Story Writing** to join in the fun. Use the guidelines and activities to write a story.

2. Select **Art Gallery** to enjoy pictures by young artists. Arthur regularly chooses new pictures to hang. He would love to see one of your pictures hanging in his gallery. Send a picture and come back to the site later to see if Arthur put it up.

3. Select **More Fun with Arthur** to have more fun with Arthur!

4. Select **Dear Arthur** to send a message to Arthur. Let him know if things you see on the Arthur show remind you of things that happen to you, if some of the Arthur stories make you laugh, and if you have ideas about what should be included in the television show or at this Web site.

5. Dictate or write a letter to Arthur and tell him about something you like about his Web pages.

_____

_____

_____

_____

_____

_____

_____

_____

Draw a picture of something you would like him to put on the Web.

Name_____

NetWork: Tell a Wacky Web Tale

Overview

Enter the world of Wacky Web Tales™ to create funny stories about you and your friends.

Procedure

With your Web browser access the URL

`http://www.hmco.com:80/hmco/school/tales`

Activities

1. Select **Mother Goose Gazette** and enter words to create a wacky tale. Enter the information requested.

   - your first and last name
   - a time
   - male friend's name
   - female friend's name
   - your school
   - plural noun
   - past tense verb
   - singular noun
   - present tense verb
   - past tense verb
   - a teacher
   - adjective

   Click **See Your Wacky Web Tale**. Here's an example:

   > Travis Burgstahler from the Mother Goose Gazette, reported that at noon, Daniel and Kelsey climbed Laurelhurst Hill to fetch a pail of action figures. All went according to plan until Daniel drove on a fish and slid down the hill. Kelsey tried to push him, but he flew past her too quickly. She then went tumbling after him.
   >
   > Mrs. T. saw what happened from the school window and raced to the bottom of the hill to see if Daniel and Lindsey were hurt. Luckily, both children were fine except for feeling a little crazy.

2. From the home page select **The Camping Trip**. After you type in the words requested you'll get a wacky story something like this:

> It was a cold, sweet night. Andrew and I flew around the campfire, swimming songs and eating bananas.
>
> Soon we got tired, climbed into our cars, and eventually fell asleep. Suddenly, we were both wide awake. There was a loud dancing sound outside the tent. I grabbed Andrew's nose and held on for dear life. Andrew started chanting, "Lions and clothes and shoes, oh my!" over and over again.
>
> Then into our tent fell our friend Marco. Marco had been thirsty and had gone into the house for some orange juice. Now the orange juice was on the floor of our tent. But we all had a good laugh and went back to sleep. It turned out to be a very blue camping trip. And maybe next time we'll even leave my backyard.

3. Select other options on the home page and have fun typing in words and reading funny stories.

4. Ask your teacher or parent to make up a funny story in which you can put the following words.

*   your name   _____

*   your city   _____

*   an animal   _____

*   a friend's name _____

*   a shape   _____

*   a toy   _____

*   a place   _____

*   a verb   _____

Now, you make up a story in which an adult or teacher can put words.

Name_____

NetWork: Visit Mr. Rogers' Neighborhood

Overview

Mr. Rogers has been a favorite television neighbor for young children for several generations. Now you can find him and his neighborhood friends on the Net.

Procedure

With your Web browser access the URL

http://www.pbs.org/rogers/

Activities

1. Select **Children's Corner**. Explore with the characters in the Neighborhood of Make Believe! Just click on a coloring page or art project, print it, and start s-t-r-e-t-c-h-i-n-g your imagination!

2. From the home page, select **Plan and Play Activities** to participate in activities with Mr. Rogers.

3. Make other selections from the home page to find more fun.

4. Write one word to describe your real neighborhood.

_____

– –

_____

5. Color this picture and the words **king** and **queen**.

VISIT OUR NEIGHBORHOOD

MISTER ROGERS' NEIGHBORHOOD

PBS ONLINE   MISTER ROGERS' NEIGHBORHOOD

king

queen

Name_____

NetWork: Alex's Scribbles

Overview

Here is a Web site that was created by a father, Scott Balson, and his young son, Alex. They live in Australia. Alex includes his own stories and pictures that help children develop reading, counting, and problem solving skills. They may inspire you to create your own Web site, but you'll need a more advanced book to take on that task.

Procedure

With your Web browser access the URL

`http://www.gil.com.au/max/`

Activities

1. Click on the picture **The Adventures of Max and Alex** to visit Max and Alex. Read through the interactive **Koala trouble stories by Alex Balson**. Enjoy Alex's click-able pictures.

2. Try some of the links for kids from **The Kids Locker Room**.

3. If you created a Web site with your mom or dad, what would you like to put on it? Dictate or write a sentence and make a picture of something you would put on your Web pages.

Name_____

✏️ NetWork: Storybooks Online

Overview

Enter a library of children's storybooks at Children's Storybooks Online.

Procedure

With your Web browser access the URL

`http://www.magickeys.com/books/`

Activities

1. Read **Buzzy Bee**. What sound does a bee make? What sound does the letter **b** make? What sound does the letter **z** make? Color the word **buzz**.

   Write the name of the person who wrote Buzzy Bee. This person is called the author of the book.

   _____

   -

   _____

2. Select **Buzzy Bee Coloring Book**. Select a picture to color. Print it on your printer and color it with crayons. Return to the home page.

3. From the home page, try **Buzzy Bee Riddles**, going to the link for the answer. Try the **Buzzy Bee Maze**, too. Return to the home page.

4. Under `Coloring Book` on the home page, select **Littlest Knight Coloring Book**. Select a picture to color. Print it on your printer and color it with crayons. Return to the home page.

5. From the home page, select other books at this site to read and enjoy. Read the name of the book and the name of the author for each. Explore other resources at this site.

6. Before leaving this Web site, be sure to check out **Related childrens story and writer/illustrator** links to find other reading resources on the Net. Write the name of one book or story and its author.

_____

\- \-

_____

\- \-

_____

7. Choose your favorite printed book. Copy the name of the book and the name of the author.

_____

\- \-

_____

\- \-

_____

Name_____

NetWork: Moo in MooTown

Overview

MooTown® is a fun place for young learners (and their companions) to visit.

Procedure

With your Web browser access the URL

`http://www.mootown.com/`

Activities

1. From the home page, select **Go to the MooTown Arcade**. Select **Spread the Words**. Dictate or type your own funny story. When finished, select **Submit** (or **Reset** if you'd rather start over or not submit at all).

2. Select other activities from the home page.

3. What sound does a cow make? Color the word.

What sounds do other animals make?

4. MooTown has an address that tells us where to find it on the Internet. Its Internet address is called a Uniform Resource Locator (URL) and looks like this:

http://www.mootown.com/

Copy all of the letters and characters in MooTown's URL.

_____

_ _

_____

Your home has an address, too. Write your street address.

_____

_ _

_____

Write the name of your city or town.

_____

_ _

_____

Write your phone number.

_____

_ _

_____

Write what you like best about where you live.

_____

_ _

_____

Name_____

▦▭▷ NetWork: Join Alice in Internetland

Overview

Do you want to share the adventures of Alice? Try out a dynamic text version of Lewis Carroll's *Alice's Adventures in Wonderland*.

Procedure

With your Web browser access the URL

`http://www.megabrands.com/alice/goalice.html`

Activities

1. Select **Online Edition** to read this classic book.

   Tell an adult what the story is about.

   Make up a song, dance, or play about an adventure that Alice might have in Wonderland. Perform for your class or family.

2. From the home page, try **Chat with Alice**.

3. Explore other areas of this site.

4. Imagine going on a trip to Wonderland. From magazines and newspapers cut out pictures of things that you might find there. Paste below to make a collage.

Name_____

▦ ▷ NetWork: Visit Seussville

Overview

Would you like to meet Dr. Seuss™? Join him in Seussville.

Procedure

With your Web browser access the URL

http://www.randomhouse.com/seussville/

Activities

1. Select **Who is Dr. Seuss?** to learn more about the author. What does it mean to be an author of a book? What does it mean to be an illustrator of a book?

2. Select **Ask the Cat** to learn more about the cat in the hat.

3. Select **Say Let's Play** to find some connect-the-dots, a maze, and games. Be sure to try the on-line games **Who Said That?** and **Oh Say Can You Say?**

4. Continue exploring this site. Write the names of Dr. Seuss characters you encounter on your Internet exploration or in printed Dr. Seuss books.

_____

- - - - - - - - - - - - - - - - - - - -

_____

_____

- - - - - - - - - - - - - - - - - - - -

_____

_____

- - - - - - - - - - - - - - - - - - - -

_____

5. Draw a picture of a favorite Dr. Seuss character.

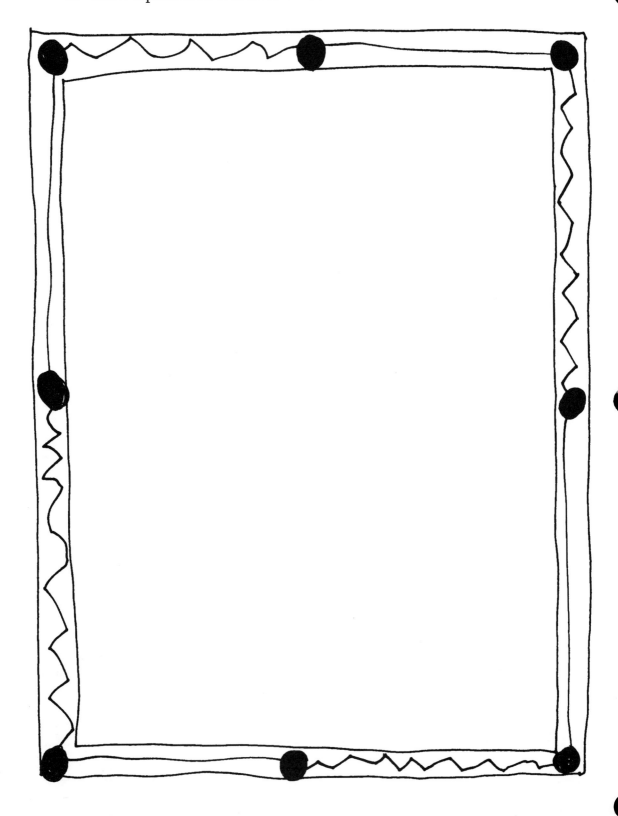

Name_____

 ## NetWork: The Brave and Bold Squirrel

Overview

Enter the world of the Red Squirrel clans and learn about a brave and bold little squirrel. The story is from *The Tales of Edgeriver Wood*.

Procedure

With your Web browser access the URL

`http://www.incwell.com/Brave/Brave.html`

Activities

1. Read the story of the brave and bold squirrel, clicking **p1**, **p2**, and so on to turn the pages in the book.

2. Print the letter that the words **brave** and **bold** begin with, lowercase on one line and uppercase on the next. What sound does the letter **b** make?

b

- -

B

- -

---

3. Write a story about an animal and draw a picture to go with it.

Name_____

NetWork: Candlelight Stories

Overview

Read colorful and engaging children's books at the Candlelight Stories™ Web site.

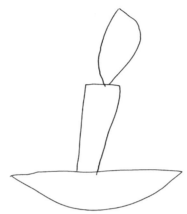

Procedure

With your Web browser access the URL

http://www.CandlelightStories.com/candle2.htm

Activities

1. In Children's Stories Illustrated select **Illustrated Mother Goose**. Read and try to contribute some of the words for these popular nursery rhymes. Re-tell the stories to an adult. Return to the home page.

2. Read other stories at this site. Tell about the stories you read. Return to the home page.

3. From the home page, select **games**. Try **The Candlelight Stories Spelling Machine**. This illustrated spelling tutor shows a picture and waits for you to type in the word on an on-screen keyboard or the computer keyboard. You can ask for the answer and erase wrong entries with a button click. When you're done, return to the home page.

4. Try other options at this site, including links to other stories and illustrated entertainment on the Web. Jot down URLs or place bookmarks where you might want to return.

5. Write a sentence about when you were a baby and draw a picture to go with it. Write your birth date.

When I was a baby I

_____

— —

_____

_____

— —

_____

Name_____

NetWork: Meet My Hero

Overview

Everybody loves a hero. Here's a chance to talk about what a hero is, who other kids look up to as heroes, and who your heroes are.

Procedure

With your Web browser access the URL

http://www.myhero.com/

Activities

Kyle is my hero.
TRAVIS

1. What is a hero?

   Choose the type of hero you would like to read about — maybe teacher hero, sports hero, or animal hero. Read some of the many hero stories.

2. Would you like to add a story about a hero to the collection? To do this, select **Tell us about your hero!**. Fill in the information requested, type in the name of your hero and answer the question Why is this your hero? Then press **Submit Hero**. Your entry will be displayed at the top of the MY HERO guest book.

3. Draw a picture of you doing something that makes you a hero.

Name_____

 NetWork: Send an Internet Greeting Card

Overview

You can save trees by designing and sending greeting cards to friends and relatives via electronic mail. Check out The Electric Postcard.

Procedure

With your Web browser access the URL

http://postcards.www.media.mit.edu/Postcards/

Activities

1. Select **Postcard Rack**. Select the type of card you wish and then the specific card. Type the electronic mail address of the recipient (If you don't know anyone's electronic mail address, send a card to yourself!). Type a subject and then a message. Type your name. Click to **Mail the postcard** or, before mailing, select **Preview the postcard**. When finished, mail the postcard.

2. Try using other sites to send greetings. Which site do you like the best?

> Awesome Cyber Cards™
> **http://www.marlo.com/**
>
> Build-A-Card
> **http://buildacard.com**
>
> Internet Greeting Cards
> **http://www.tenn.com/igc/lettershort.html**

3. It is important to communicate regularly with our friends and family, even if they live far away. There are many different ways that people can send greetings to one another. Tell what you like and dislike about communicating in these ways:

   - by telephone
   - using postal mail
   - via electronic mail
   - in person

4. Create a postcard with an address and message on one side and a picture on the other. If you use cardboard, you can cut out your postcard and mail it to a friend. Don't forget the postage stamp!

Front:

Back:

Name_____

NetWork: McGuffie Avenue Gang

Overview

Join the McGuffie Avenue gang for some fun.

Procedure

With your Web browser access the URL

http://www.mcguffie.on.ca/

Activities

1. Click on characters in the picture to learn about them.

    Click the **HOME** icon to return to the home page.

2. From the home page, select **ADVENTURES IN CRANBERRY FOREST** to preview the magical, musical world of McGuffie Avenue.

    Return to the home page.

3. Select **FUN AND GAMES** to complete a **Dot-to-Dot** and **The Amazing McGuffie Maze**. Print the activities on your printer.

    Return to the home page.

4. Before leaving this site, from the home page select **OTHER GREAT LINKS** to explore other Web sites for kids.

5. Dictate or write a story and draw a picture about your friends.

Name_____

NetWork: Kody's Beary Scary Story

Overview

Join a bear named Kody on an adventure in the Smoky Mountains. Read great stories, learn interesting things, and participate in fun activities at "Kody's Home" Page.

Procedure

With your Web browser access the URL

http://www.usit.net/public/johncg/Kody/KodyPage.HTML

Activities

1. Select **Kody's Beary Scary Story** and help Kody through some tight spots if you're brave enough! Make choices about the direction of the story. Return to the home page.

2. From the home page select **Did you know...** to learn some interesting stuff. Return to the home page.

3. From the home page select **Hopping good dot to dot** to print a puzzle to complete. Return to the home page.

4. From the home page try **Visit some places Kody likes to visit** to link to some other interesting sites. Make a note of the URLs or save bookmarks for sites to which you would like to return.

5. What sound does the letter **b** make? What sound does the letter **r** make? Color the word **bear**, each letter a different color. Draw a picture of Kody in a scene from the story you read.

Name_____

⬛▭▭▷ NetWork: Safety First!

Overview

You'll find lots of pictures to color on the Web. Check out a large collection of coloring pages at Mac's Colouring Book Pages.

Procedure

With your Web browser access the URL

http://www.compunik.com/kidesign/karen/coloring.htm

Activities

1. Choose pictures from a collection of safety topics, including:

   • Visit the Dentist
   • Outside Safety
   • Fire Safety
   • School Bus Safety

   Write a sentence about something you do to stay safe.

_____

- -

_____

- -

_____

- -

_____

- -

_____

2. Print and color pictures in the `Zoo Animals` area. Write the name of one animal.

_____

- -

_____

3. Try the fun coloring pages of Disney, Star Wars, Oliver and Company, Space Jam, Garfield and other characters. Dictate or write a story about your favorite character.

_____

- -

_____

_____

- -

_____

_____

- -

_____

_____

- -

_____

_____

- -

_____

Name_____

NetWork: Meet Theodore Tugboat

Overview

Theodore Tugboat™ is a Canadian television series. At the Theodore Tugboat Online Activity Centre you can participate in interactive stories where you make choices about the story direction, print pictures to color, and more.

Procedure

With your Web browser access the URL

> **http://www.cochran.com/theodore**

Activities

1. From the THINGS TO DO WITH US menu select **interactive stories** and then select a story. Learn about the characters and make choices about the story direction. Try another story.

2. From the THINGS TO DO WITH US menu select **Characters** to learn more about the characters and the functions of different types of boats.

3. From the THINGS TO DO WITH US menu select **Colouring Book**. Follow the instructions to download pictures to color.

Here's a picture of Petra to color with real coloring crayons. Draw a
picture of you standing on Petra's deck.

4. From the THINGS TO DO WITH US menu select **Berit's Best
   Sites for Children** to explore other World Wide Web sites for
   kids. You could be caught in this Web collection for a very long time.

Name_____

NetWork: Get Caught in a Kids' Net

Overview

Ponyshow's Kids is an activity center for young children. It includes lots of fun things to see and do, including art projects, a gallery, a story contest, puzzles, and much more.

Procedure

With your Web browser access the URL

http://www.PonyShow.com/KidsNet/website.htm

Activities

1. Select the **CLICK ME** icon to meet Pennywinkle and learn about the Rastakans. Click **write** to send her an electronic mail message about yourself.

    Click **Home** to return to the home page.

2. Select the **Super's Studio** icon. See art by kids and find fun art projects you can do yourself.

    Click **Home** to return to the home page.

3. Select **Bamboozle's BookNook** to find lots of books, book reviews by kids, original stories, and more.

    Click **Home** to return to the home page.

4. If you like puzzles and games, select **Paradox's Puzzles** from the home page.

    Click **Home** to return to the home page.

5. Click on other characters and activities from the home page. Have fun with this rich set of resources.

    Before you leave Ponyshow's Kids, click the **Lightfoot's Software Loft** icon to explore links to other kids' sites on the Internet.

6. Dictate or write a story about your next birthday. How old will you be? Decorate your cake. Don't forget the candles.

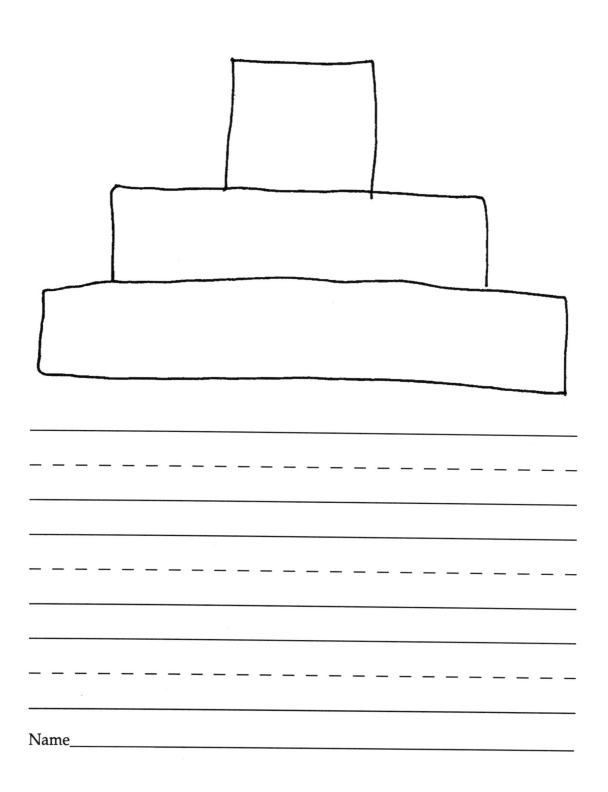

Name_____

NetWork: Visit the Platypus Family Playroom

Overview

Visit a family's playroom where they've collected stories, games, mazes, and songs. Activities are available in English or Spanish.

Procedure

With your Web browser access the URL

`http://www.orst.edu/~dickt/playroom/playroom.html`

Activities

1. Select **stories** to read stories written by Platypus family friends. Try puzzles, games, and other activities at this site. If you have the necessary hardware and software, you can even hear songs.

2. Families read together, play together, and work together. Draw yours:

- reading together.

- playing together.

- working together.

3. On each line, write the name of a person or pet in your family.

_____

- -

_____

_____

- -

_____

_____

- -

_____

_____

- -

_____

_____

- -

_____

Circle the name that has the most letters.

Circle the name that has the fewest letters.

Name_____

NetWork: International Kids' Space

Overview

International Kids' Space is everybody's home page! Enjoy an activity center, galleries of art and music by kids, and stories written by children.

Procedure

With your Web browser access the URL

http://www.kids-space.org/

Activities

1. Select **Guide Bear's Guide Tour**. Select **Tip the Bear's Tips**. Read through the instructions in this and other sections.

   Click the **Kids' Space** icon to return to the home page.

2. From the home page, select **Story Book**. Explore activities that are of the kids, by the kids, and for the kids.

   Click the **Kids' Space** icon to return to the home page.

3. From the home page, select **Beanstalk** to have fun in the Craft Room.

   Click the **Kids' Space** icon to return to the home page.

4. From the home page, select **Kids' Gallery**. View pictures and stories by other children. Write a story for your favorite picture and check out the instructions for submitting it.

5. Try a few other options from the home page.

6. You can also **illustrate** a story in the storybook and enter it.
    Practice below. Read the instructions for submission.

Name_____

 ## NetWork: Ride the Bus with Curious George

Overview

Enter the World of Curious George, the Internet home of a curious chimp.

Procedure

With your Web browser access the URL

`http://www.hmco.com/hmco/trade/hmi/george/game/`

Activities

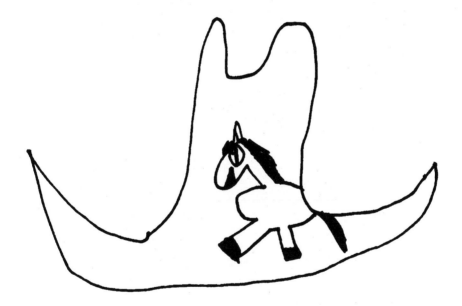

1. Click on the person you want George to either take or give a hat. Continue making choices as you work through the activity.

2. Make a picture of you and the other members of your family, each wearing a hat.

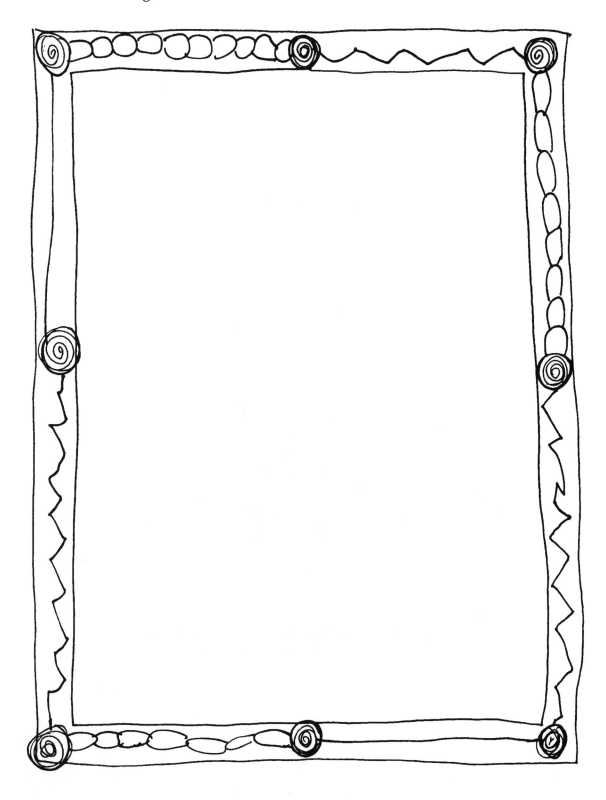

Name_____

NetWork: The Prince and I

Overview

Go on an exciting mission to deliver a secret message to the Prince. Play scrambled words, rhyme time, magic squares, and more.

Procedure

With your Web browser access the URL

`http://www.nfb.ca/Kids/`

Activities

1. Choose the option to take a trip around the **kingdom** with the Queen. The Queen will tell you about a little Prince who decided not to go to school. Options appear at the bottom of the screen. Explore.

2. In the `Reading Coach` section, choose **Rhyme Time** and find the word that rhymes with the picture in the box.

   Choose **Magic Squares** to drag and drop magic squares and solve puzzles.

   Choose **SCRAMBLED WORDS** to drag and drop letters to make words.

3. Click on the telescope icon to find out about the Prince, specifically, **What's He Up To?**

4. From the home page choose the option to **Become the Prince's friend** if you want to be able to have a home page with your own picture, see your name in stories and games, have stories e-mailed to you, or go on a treasure hunt.

5. In the `Show and Tell` area, choose **Happy Herald** to develop a story of your very own.

   Choose **Tell a tall tale** to write a story and send it to the Prince.

   Choose **Picture us together** to learn how to send a picture to the Prince.

Choose **Art Jems** to learn how to send your drawing to the Prince. Practice below.

Name_____

 ## NetWork: Publish or Perish

Overview

KidPub was developed by a parent who wanted to encourage his daughter to write stories. KidPub gives you a place to share your work with other kids.

Procedure

With your Web browser access the URL

    http://www.kidpub.org/kidpub/

Activities

1. Select **Questions and Answers** to learn more about KidPub. Go **Back to KidPub**.

2. Check out **Newest Stories**, **Older Stories (but goodies!)**, **Search all KidPub Stories**, and **KidPub Publisher's Picks** to read stories written by children from around the world. Choose stories by younger contributors to see what children your age write about. Go **Back to KidPub**.

3. Select **How to Publish Your Story** to learn how to send stories to KidPub. Travis, age 6, submitted the following story and information about himself.

> A lion's best friend
> by Travis, age 6
>
> A tiger was walking in the forest and he saw a lion trapped in a trap. The tiger helped the lion by chewing on the rope of the trap with his teeth. After the lion was out of the trap he thanked the tiger for saving him from the hunters. The end.

> My name is Travis. I live in Seattle. I have two gerbils named Cookie and Brownie. I have two fish named Elvis and Goldie. I like to play baseball.

4. Now it's your turn. Submit a story by following the instructions in
   How to Publish Your Story. If you don't want to submit a story
   now or you want to practice first, write a story on the lines below.

Name_____

NetWork: Stop for Tea with Hello Kitty

Overview

Join Hello Kitty and Bear for tea and make important choices along the way.

Procedure

With your Web browser access the URL

`http://www.users.dircon.co.uk/~seenoise/kitty/hellokit.htm`

Activities

1. Choose what type of tea you would like to drink, whether you would like sugar and milk, and what biscuit you want to eat. Click the button **Tell Hello Kitty** once you have made your choices. Help Bear choose what to wear to the tea party by clicking on the outfit you like best. Enjoy the tea party with Hello Kitty and Bear. You can even find some yummy recipes.

   Press **Start Hello Kitty's tea party again** if you want to make more choices.

2. Write your name, Hello Kitty, and Bear. Then make a picture of the three of you drinking tea.

3. Plan a tea party with your family at your home.

Name_____

NetWork: Welcome to the White House

Overview

It's never too early to learn about our government. The White House Web pages include a special place for young people. This activity refers to the Web site of the Whitehouse during the Clinton administration.

Procedure

With your Web browser access the URL

`http://www.whitehouse.gov/WH/kids/html/home.html`

Activities

1. You will be greeted by Socks.

Welcome to the White House for Kids

Hi. My name is Socks. I am a member of the Clinton family. I will be your guide to the White House web site. If this is your first time here, begin your adventure by clicking on my picture below.

1. Select **White House Kids** to learn about children of presidents who have lived in the White House. Return to `The White House for Kids` home page.

2. Select **White House Pets** to learn about animals that have lived in the White House. What kind of pets have lived in the White House? Draw a picture of a dog and a cat and color the words.

dog cat

Name_____

 ## NetWork: Story Time

Overview

You'll find lots of stories on the Internet to read or download. Some of them are from well-known printed books. Some can be found only on the Net. Read *Silly Billy* stories, *Mother Goose, Alice in Wonderland, Wizard of Oz*, and more.

Procedure

With your Web browser access the URLs

The BookWire Electronic Children's Books Index
http://www.bookwire.com/links/readingroom/
        echildbooks.html

Classics for Young People
http://www.ucalgary.ca/~dkbrown/storclas.html

Concertina
http://www.iatech.com/books/

Grandad's Animal Alphabet Book - K to 3
http://www.mrtc.org/~twright/animals/grandad.htm

Online Children's Stories
http://www.ucalgary.ca/~dkbrown/stories.html

Online Children's STORIES
http://www.intex.net/~dlester/pam/stories/stories.html

The Page at Pooh Corner
http://www.public.iastate.edu/~jmilne/pooh.html

Peter Pan
gopher://wiretap.spies.com:70/00/Library/Classic/
        peter.txt/

Silly Billys World
http://www.sillybilly.com/

Where's Waldo
http://www.warneractive.com/Imagination_Pilots/
        Waldo/Docs/wwb.html

Activities

In many stories you learn about children and animals trying new things. Sometimes they do well and sometimes they need to practice.

1. Make a picture of something you do well.

2. Make a picture of something that you want to learn to do better.

Name_____

Chapter Three
NetWork for Young Learners:
Science, Mathematics

Notes to Teachers and Parents

Some resources on the Internet help young learners explore basic mathematics and science concepts.

Prerequisites

In order to complete the NetWork in this chapter you will need access to a computer, the Internet network, and World Wide Web browser software.

Objectives

After completion of the NetWork in this chapter young learners will be able to use the keyboard and mouse to perform basic functions on the computer and the World Wide Web. They will use Internet resources to learn about science and mathematics. Completion of the activities will help young children learn to:

- count objects,
- identify numerals,
- write numerals,
- compare (e.g., more/less/equal, heavier/lighter, bigger/smaller, longer/shorter),
- demonstrate the concepts of addition and subtraction,
- extend a given pattern,
- sort objects (e.g., by size, shape, color),
- identify positions (e.g., above, between, beside),
- identify shapes (e.g., circle, square, triangle, rectangle, oval, diamond, curved line, straight line),
- measure objects given a unit of measure, and
- classify (e.g., plant/animal, girl/boy).

Student Activities

1. Review all materials in this chapter. Test activities. Edit and expand upon worksheets as appropriate for your children.

2. Choose appropriate NetWork worksheets; work through the exercises with the children, maximizing their participation. Read instructions to them or help them read. For writing exercises, children can do the writing or dictate to an adult, the scribe. Talk to them about their discoveries.

3. Extend the exercises and create more activities as appropriate.

References

Chapter Six lists on-line resources for further exploration of the Internet. *Chapter Seven* includes ideas for creating additional NetWork.

✏️ NetWork: Under the Sea

Overview

Learn about whales, dolphins, turtles, otters, sharks, and more at Wyland Kid's Web.

Procedure

With your Web browser access the URL

`http://www.wylandkids.com/`

Activities

1. Select **About Wyland** to learn more about this site and explore under-the-sea resources.

2. Select **Coloring Book** and select some marine life pictures to color. Print the coloring pages on your printer. Learn some interesting facts about the marine life pictured. Talk about what you see and learn.

3. Circle the biggest marine life and draw a picture of it to the right.

dolphin

whale

clam

turtle

shark

salmon

eel

crab

4. Learn more about marine life at the Fish Information Service (FINS) with URL

    http://www.actwin.com/fish/

5. What is an aquarium? Visit an aquarium on-line. For example,

    Florida Aquarium
    http://www.sptimes.com/aquarium/

    The Monterey Bay Aquarium
    http://www.mbayaq.org/

Draw fish in the aquarium. Color the letters in the word.

aquarium

Name_____

✏️ NetWork: Soar with the Airplanes

Overview

Learn about Jay Jay® the Jet Plane and his airplane buddies. Select, print, and color pictures.

Procedure

With your Web browser access the URL

http://www.jayjay.com/

Activities

1. Select **bedtime story** and learn more about Jay Jay. Return to the home page.

2. From the home page select **Jay Jay**, **Snuffy**, and other names to send messages to your favorite characters. Return to the home page.

3. From the home page, select **Coloring book**.

Select a picture. Print it on your printer and color it.

4. Color Jay Jay and Big Jake flying piggyback.

In this picture, how many tails does each plane have? How many tails altogether? How many wings does each plane have? How many wings do the two plane have altogether? How many windows does each plane have? How many windows do they have altogether?

Name_____

🖎 NetWork: Mr. Flibby

Overview

Learn about a man whose very long arms create interesting problems to solve.

Procedure

With your Web browser access the URL

http://home.navisoft.com/bcd/flibcov.htm

Activities

1. Select **Click Here to start the Adventure**. Click to turn the pages of this electronic book.

2. Color the word **long**. How many letters are in this word?

3. Circle the name of the part of your body which is the longest. Put an **x** on the name of the part of your body which is the shortest.

foot   hand   finger   toe   leg   arm

4. Pretend you have very long arms. Draw a picture of yourself doing something that would be easier for you to do if your arms were longer than they are now. Dictate or write a sentence about the picture.

Name_____

◼▷ NetWork: Bean Time

Overview

Visit the fantasy Island of Meddybemps where Beano Sapien jelly bean people live. You'll have fun at the Chateau Meddybemps™ site on the World Wide Web.

Procedure

With your Web browser access the URL

http://www.meddybemps.com/

Activities

1. Select **Click here** to see a large panoramic view of the island of Meddybemps and to read stories. Click **Return** to go back to the Chateau Meddybemps home page.

2. Click **Beantime Stories** to enter Tippity Witchet's Beantime Stories. Scroll through the page. Count the number of pictures of people you find. Write the number.

   _____

   _ _ _ _ _ _ _ _ _

   _____

2. Click **Frogwart and the Tooth Fairies** to learn a very funny thing about tooth fairies.

   Click **Next Page** to turn the pages in this electronic book.

   Click **Beantime Stories** to return to the Tippity Witchet's Beantime Stories page.

3. Click **The Legend of Chateau Meddybemps™** to learn about Tippity Witchet. Return to the Tippity Witchet's Beantime Stories page.

4. Click **Learning Activities**. You'll find lots of problem-solving activities. For example, the section on fire engines begins like this:

What's different about these fire engines?

How many fire engines are there?

What color are they?

How many firemen are on each fire engine?

Who else is going for a ride?

Scroll down for MORE

Try the activities about trains, clowns, and hats. Be sure to say "choo choo choo" for the train when you make it scroll across the screen. And, be careful to get the hats on the right people!

Name_____

NetWork: Hop on the Magic School Bus

Overview

Explore Scholastic's The Magic School Bus™ Fun Place, based on the award-winning book series by Joanna Cole and Bruce Degen. The stories feature a wacky science teacher named Ms. Frizzle who takes her class on educational field trips in her magic bus.

Procedure

With your Web browser access the URL

> `http://scholastic.com/`

Activities

1. Under `Books` on the `Scholastic Place` page, select **The Magic School Bus** to enter `The Magic School Bus Fun Place`. Select **art gallery** to view art work of other children and enter your own. Return to the home page.

   Select **Bus News** or **Cool Stuff** to find more fun. Return to the home page.

   Select **neat games** to print a mystery name search puzzle, print a picture to color, and participate in other activities.

   Miss Frizzle weighs about 100 pounds. For each of the following items, circle **more** if the object ways more than 100 pounds and **less** if it weighs less.

The school bus	more	less
One of the students	more	less
A classroom chair	more	less
A beehive	more	less
The earth	more	less
A butterfly	more	less

2. Return to the `Scholastic Place` home page. Explore other books and offerings.

3. Draw pictures of you and your friends in a school bus.

Name_____

NetWork: Space Coloring Book

Overview

Discover aeronautics and space as you enjoy coloring at a NASA Web site.

Procedure

With your Web browser access the URL

`http://tommy.jsc.nasa.gov/~woodfill/SPACEED/`
`SEHHTML/color.html`

Activities

SPACE COLORING BOOK

Discover Aeronautics and Space
A Coloring Book for Elementary Students

National Aeronautics and Space Administration
Washington, D.C. 20546

PED-118/4-90

HTML Adaptation by Jerry Woodfill
NASA Johnson Space Center
Houston, TX 77058

1. From LIST OF PICTURES, choose a picture to view, print, and color. Information about its contents is provided for each. Talk about each picture with a parent or teacher. Have fun learning about space and aeronautics side-by-side.

2.   Color the lunar rover vehicle.

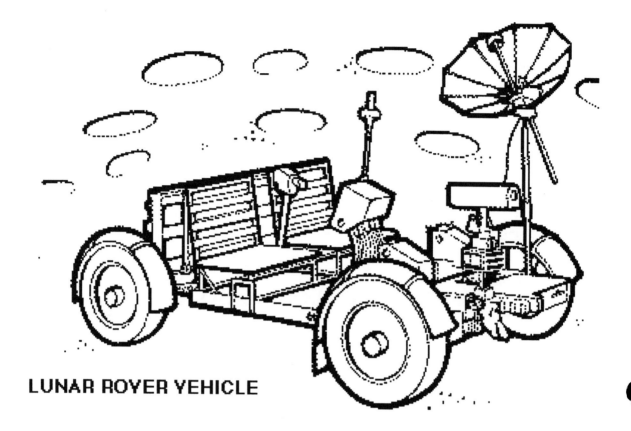

LUNAR ROVER VEHICLE

a.   What was the Lunar Rover Vehicle used for?

b.   Who used the Lunar Rover Vehicle?

c.   How did the Lunar Rover Vehicle get to the moon?

d.   Color the letters. Say the sound that each letter makes.

Name_____

✏️➤ NetWork: Beautiful Butterflies

Overview

Learn about butterflies and other science topics in Kid's Corner, a Web site of the United States Geological Survey.

Procedure

With your Web browser access the URL

> `http://www.nbs.gov/features/kidscorner/index.html`

Activities

1. Select **Children's Butterfly Site**. Select **coloring page** to learn about the life cycle of the Monarch. Learn about how you can raise a caterpillar.

2. Select pictures to print and color. Try this one for starters.

3. Visit the **Gallery** of butterfly photographs. Select **Web Sites with butterfly pictures** and **World Wide Web Sites** to continue exploring the world of the butterfly.

4. Select **Go to Exploring Science** to find other science adventures for children.

Name_____

NetWork: KidsXone

Overview

The KidsXone site in Singapore features the Adventures of Hip-O, a curious green Hippopotamus who enjoys traveling. Meet Captain Quest, compute with the Evil Mathematician, and learn some funny jokes.

Procedure

With your Web browser access the URL

`http://www.mediacity.com.sg/kidsxone/`

Activities

1. Select **The Adventures of Hip-O**. Learn with Hip-O. He is curious and loves to travel. Click **Return to KidXone** to return to the home page.

2. Select **Captain Quest and the Evil Mathematician!** He'll help you learn math the fun way. Click **Return to KidXone** to return to the home page.

   What is a mathematician? You met the Evil Mathematician. Now you can be a mathematician yourself. Practice measuring and counting.

   Measure some things in your house by using your own body.

   How many of your feet is it from the kitchen sink to the refrigerator? _____

   How many of your feet is it from your bed to the bathroom? _____

   How many hands tall is a cereal box? _____

   How many hands tall is your bed? _____

   How many of your whole body lengths are as long as your bedroom? _____

In your house, count the number of these things.

Windows   _____   **Chairs**   _____

Doors   _____   **Beds**   _____

---

3. Select **Jokes** to read some funny jokes. Tell a joke that your friends would think is funny. Here's an example from 6-year-old Travis:

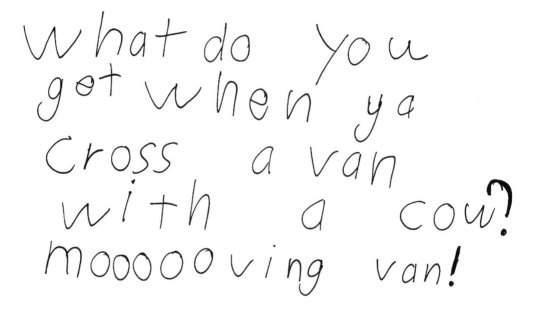

What do you get when ya cross a van with a cow? moooooving van!

mooving van

4. Try other options at this site. Before you leave, be sure to select **Surfing Points for Kids** to find other places on the Internet you will enjoy visiting.

Name_____

NetWork: Animals in Australia

Overview

Children in Australia created the activities at the Wangaratta Primary School Web site.

Procedure

With your Web browser access the URL

http://www.ozemail.com.au/~wprimary/wps.htm

It will be helpful to have a printed map of the world.

Activities

1. Select **Fun Aussie activities !!** to learn about Australian animals while you participate in fun activities. Word search, dot-to-dot, coloring – they're all here! Click the **Home Page** button when you're done with the activities.

2. Select **Meet Matthew!** to learn about one of the students working on the project; he's a real "Net Guru."

3. Look at a printed map and find out where Australia is. How far is this country from where you live? Look at the home page to find out in which city Wangaratta Primary School is. How many people live there? How many students are in the school? How old are they? How does the school compare with the school you attend or a school in your neighborhood?

4. If you made a Web site for your home or school, write or dictate one thing you would put on it? Why would children from around the world want to come to your site?

_____

_ _

_____

5. Draw a map of Australia and write the word **Australia**. On the map show pictures of animals that live in Australia.

Name_____

NetWork: Find Your Rainbow

Overview

Travel to Rainbow Land to listen to songs, print pictures to color, read a rhyming story, and download a coloring book.

Procedure

With your Web browser access the URL

http://members.aol.com/RainboLand/index.htm

Activities

1. Select **Read About Rainbow Land** for a story and pretty pictures.

    Click **Return to the Rainbow Land home page**.

2. From the home page select **Print out pages to color** to print pictures of animals in Rainbow Land to color with your own coloring crayons.

    Click **Return to the Rainbow Land home page**.

3. Select **More a-MAZE-ing new fun to print out**. Choose the size of the maze you would like to solve. Follow the instructions to complete the maze.

    Click **Return to the Rainbow Land home page**.

4. Try other activities at this site.

5. Draw a picture of a rainbow and copy the letters in the word.

r a i n b o w

Name_____

NetWork: Build a Monster

Overview

Build your own monster? You sure can – at the Build-a-Monster site on the Web.

Procedure

With your Web browser access the URL

http://www.rahul.net/renoir/monster/monster.html

Activities

1. Select a body part and you will be given several choices to replace it. Click on your choice. How do you like the monster you created? Build another one.

2. Make your own build-a-monster game. In the rectangles on the back of this sheet, draw four creatures – head in top box, torso and arms in middle box and feet in bottom box. Here are a couple of examples.

Cut out the rectangles and arrange in funny ways to make your own monsters.

NetWork: Join Billy Bear in the Playground

Overview

Billy Bear says his playground is a place where kids can be kids, and parents and teachers... well... yeah... they can come play too! And, your parents will be happy to know that the only dirt you'll see is when Billy makes his fabulous mud pies.

Procedure

With your Web browser access the URL

http://www.worldvillage.com/kidz/

Activities

1. From the `WorldVillage Kidz` home page, select **BILLY BEAR** to enter Billy Bear's Playground.

2. Select **ABOUT BILLY BEAR** to learn about Billy Bear.

   Who is he?

   Who created him?

   Where is he from?

   Who are some of his friends?

   What does he like to do?

   Return to **Billy Bear's HomePage**.

3. Select **BILLY BEAR STORYBOOKS** to learn about how you can obtain some shareware storybooks to run on your own computer. Return to **Billy Bear's HomePage**.

4. Select **HOW TO MAKE YOUR STORYBOOK** to learn about how you can create your own animated storybook. Return to **Billy Bear's HomePage**.

5. Select **FREE FUN & GAMES** to find some on-line and paper games. Here is an example of an activity you can print and complete.

    Return to **Billy Bear's HomePage**.

6. Explore other areas of Billy Bear's Playground. Before you leave this site, be sure to try **MORE HOT SITES**.

7. Create an activity like some of the those you found in Billy Bear's Playground that other children could complete. For example, one six-year-old came up with this idea.

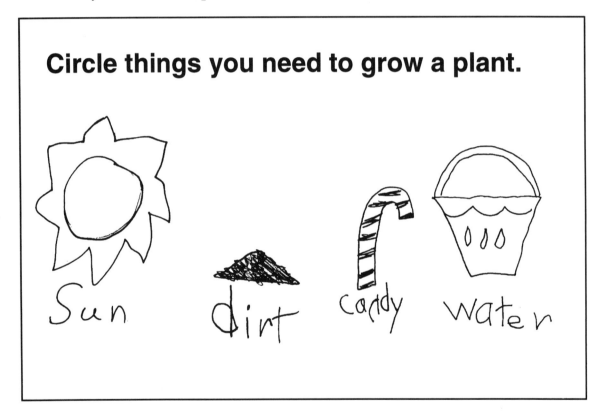

Circle things you need to grow a plant.

Sun   dirt   candy   water

Now, grow a real plant at your home!

Name_____

NetWork: Dream about the Dinosaurs

Overview

All kids, including little Web explorers, love to learn about dinosaurs. Knowledge Adventure™ maintains the Jump Start Kids Dinosaur Activity Center.

Procedure

With your Web browser access the URL

`http://www.adventure.com/kids/dinosaurs`

Activities

1. Select **CONNECT THE DOTS** to go to an on-line connect-the-dots activity. Click on the numbers to finish the picture. Select other pictures to complete. Go back to the DINOSAURS home page.

2. Select **COLORING BOOK** to color pictures of dinosaurs on-line. Click on a color; try a different color and see what happens. Choose other pictures to color on-line. Go back to the DINOSAURS home page.

3. Select **CREATE-A-SAURUS** to create your own dinosaur. Select the dinosaur type and skin design.

4. Select **STICKER BOOK** to select and position stickers in a sticker book on-line.

5. Draw a picture of a dinosaur.

Name_____

✏️ NetWork: Jump Start Elementary

Overview

Jump Start Grade School by Knowledge Adventure™ is fun for young learners, toddlers through second grade.

Procedure

With your Web browser access the URL

http://www.adventure.com/kids/jumpstart/

Activities

1. Select **Preschool**. Click on the appropriate icons to try sticker, connect-the-dots, puzzle, matching and coloring activities. Go back to the Jump Start Grade School home page.

2. From the Jump Grade School home page, select **Toddlers** to find activities for the younger set. Click on icons to try sticker, telling time, puzzle, and coloring activities. Go back to the Jump Start Grade School home page.

3. From the home page, select **Kindergarten, 1st. Grade,** or **2nd. Grade** to find more activities at these levels. Go back to the Jump Start Grade School home page.

4. From the home page, select **Casper** to enter the haunted Whipstaff Manor. Click on **Casper** again to go to Casper's Coloring Page. Then, click on the color you want to use and the area you want colored. Go back to the Jump Start Grade School home page.

5. From the home page, select **Movie Theater** to color a superhero. Go back to the Jump Start Grade School home page.

6. Check out other activity areas at this site.

7. Draw a picture of Casper and two of his ghostly friends. Color Casper's name.

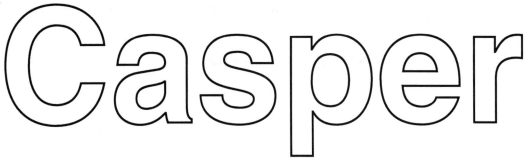

Name_____

NetWork: Zoom to the Zoo

Overview

Do you like to visit the zoo? Visit the zoo animals at ZooNet™ for Kids.

Procedure

With your Web browser access the URL

http://members.aol.com/zoonetkids/index.htm

Activities

1. From the `ZooNet for Kids` home page, select **Trek Kids**. Now you're at the `Northwest Trek` site. Read through the `Can you guess what kind of animal I am?` section. You can submit by electronic mail the names of animals you encounter in your neighborhood or in the woods.

   Go back to the `ZooNet` home page.

2. From the `ZooNet` home page under `Children's Zoo Pages`, select some children's zoos to explore. Your choices include sites sponsored by:

   > The Micke Grove Zoo
   > Metro Washington Park Zoo
   > The Sedgwick County Zoo
   > The Phoenix Zoo
   > The New England Aquarium
   > Knoxville Zoo
   > Northwest Trek Animal Park

   After each exploration, go back to the `ZooNet` home page.

3. Explore other sections of the `ZooNet` site.

4. Explore other sites that feature animals. The following list provides some examples.

The BoomerWolf™ Page
`http://www.boomerwolf.com/`

The Cub Den
`http://www.nature-net.com/bears/cubden.html`

The Froggy Page
`http://frog.simplenet.com/froggy/`

Grandad's Animal Alphabet Book
`http://www.mrtc.org/~twright/animals/grandad.htm`

Herp Pictures
`http://gto.ncsa.uiuc.edu/pingleto/lobby.html`

Family Surfboard's A Net Full of Animals
`http://www.familysurf.com/act2.htm`

Our Penguin Fact Book
`http://www.cpcs.K12.ny.us/Penguins/Book.html`

Select-a-Dog
`http://earth.myriad.net/dogs/dogindex.html/`

Whale Times Kid's Page
`http://www.whaletimes.org/whakids.htm`

Zoo in the Wild
`http://ape.apenet.it/EDV/ZOO/n_ing.html`

---

5. What is a zoo? What can you find there? Have you been to a zoo?

6. Collect stuffed and plastic animals in your home or school. Use boxes and other materials to create a zoo., arranging similar animals together. Pretend to be the zoo keeper. Invite friends and family to visit your zoo.

Name_____

 NetWork: Recycle

Overview

Have fun coloring as you learn about recycling at the GREEN VALLEY Recycling Coloring Book site.

Procedure

With your Web browser access the URL

`http://www.greenvalley.com/coloring/colorme1.html`

Activities

1. Choose a picture to print and color. Name the shapes that you find in the picture.

2. Color this recycle picture with coloring crayons. Next to the recycling driver, draw some things that you can recycle from your home.

MEET YOUR RECYCLING DRIVER. HE WILL HELP YOU RECYCLE.

Name_____

NetWork: Stroll Down Sesame Street

Overview

Visit Sesame Street™ characters on the Net.

Procedure

With your Web browser access the URL

`http://www.pbs.org/kids/sesame/`

Activities

1. Select **STORYBOOK** for to read a Sesame Street story. Return to the Sesame Street home page.

2. From the COLORING area, choose **Shapes** to learn about shapes. Here's an example of what you'll find:

3. From the COLORING area, choose **Numbers** to print pages to color. In this one, count the apples with Cookie Monster and Betty Lou.

4. From the COLORING area, select **Alphabet** to print pages that help you learn your A, B, C's. Return to the Sesame Street home page.

5. For more Sesame Street activities visit the Childrens' Television Workshop™ pages by clicking on **CTW's website**.

Name_____

◼▭▷ NetWork: Mr. Edible Starchy Tuber Head

Overview

Mr. Edible Starchy Tuber Head, who has an amazing resemblance to Mr. Potatohead™, is an active guy on the Net.

Procedure

With your Web browser access the URL

http://winnie.acsu.buffalo.edu/potatoe/

Activities

1. Try the many options on this page. The list looks something like this:

```
              Incredible Potatoe Stuff
Our favorite fan mail.
Really cute Mr. Potato Head Halloween Costume
Mr. Edible Starchy Tuber Head Goes to Hollywood
Our cohorts over in Networking don't get out much.
Mr. ESTH - the Authorized Biography.
Mr ESTH makes friends at USENIX LISA Conference '95
Mr. Edible Starchy Tuber Head Source
PotatoeCam- Updated when the mood strikes.
PotatoeCam Hall of Fame
Mr. Edible Starchy Tuber Head's Worst Nightmare
If you like Mr. Edible Starchy Tuber Head, let us know!

            For Netscape version 1.1 and up:
Mr. Edible Starchy Tuber Head for Web Potatoes
The Evolution of Mr. Edible Starchy Tuber Head
The Amazing Flying Edible Starchy Tuber Head
International Versions
Pig Latin
Canadian!
```

2. Try some other "Mr. Potatohead" sites listed under `Other Potato Games on the Web`.

3. Use a real potato and other objects from your kitchen to create a Mr. Potatohead.

4. Color this Mr. Potatohead that was drawn by a 6-year-old child. On a separate piece of paper, draw and color Mr. or Mrs. Potatohead.

5. Create a Mr. or Mrs. Potatohead out of a real potato.

Name_____

⬛➤ NetWork: Crayola

Overview

Interested in coloring? Try the Crayola home page. You can learn how crayolas are made, absorb some crayola trivia, find some stain removal tips, learn about crayola history, and take part in some on-line activities.

Procedure

With your Web browser access the URL

`http://www.crayola.com/crayola/crayons/home.html`

Activities

1. Learn how crayolas are made by reading the information provided at this site. You may also enjoy crayola history and trivia.

2. Try the activities offered. They change periodically.

3. Draw a pile of crayolas on top of the one below. Color them.

4. Now that you've played with virtual crayolas, create a picture with
    real crayons.

Name_____

NetWork: Tackle Tic Tac Toe

Overview

Tic Tac Toe is a fun game to play, even with a computer! Warning: the computer is a VERY good player.

Procedure

With your Web browser access the URL

http://www.bu.edu/Games/tictactoe

Activities

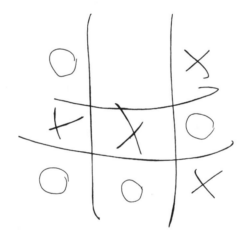

1. You will be **X**. The computer will be **o**. Try to get three **X**'s in a row.

    Select **You go first**. Click the square in which you want your **X**.

2. What is the shape of the Tic Tac Toe board? How many squares is it wide? How many squares high is it? How many squares are in the board altogether?

3. Color TIC TAC TOE on the next page. How many **T**'s are in Tic Tac Toe? How many **C**'s? How many **E**'s? How many letters all together? Which letters have curved lines? Which have straight lines?

4. On a different sheet of paper, play Tic Tac Toe with a teacher, parent, brother, sister, or friend.

Name_____

 **NetWork: Visit Coco and Loco**

Overview

It is claimed that cats Coco and Loco created the Coco and Loco Cat Page Hall of Fame for all of the cats out there who rack up time on their owners' Internet accounts when everyone is asleep, in school, or at work. Coco and Loco work on the page in their spare time between eating and sleeping.

Procedure

With your Web browser access the URL

    http://www.nomius.com/~cocoloco/c-and-l.htm

Activities

1. Select **Go to the gallery**. Look at pictures and read stories about cats.

    Return to the home page.

2. From the home page select **Other related sites** and surf the Net.

    Return to the home page.

3. From the home page select **Send us your comments**. Type your impressions of the site and recommendations for additions.

4. If you have a cat, you can send a photo with a brief biography to be included at the site.

5. Do you think the cats Coco and Loco really made this Web site? If not, who do you think did?

6. If you have a cat in your family or know a cat owned by a neighbor or
   friend, draw a picture of the cat. Or, just draw a picture of a cat that
   you would like to have for a pet someday. Write the name of the cat.

Name

NetWork: Endangered Species

Overview

In Kid's Corner learn what it means to be an endangered species and why it's important to protect species that are endangered.

Procedure

With your Web browser access the URL

`http://www.nbs.gov/features/kidscorner/index.html`

Activities

1. Select **Endangered Species**. What does it mean to be an endangered species? Why is it important to protect species that are endangered? Talk about endangered species with your parent or teacher. Select **Return to the Kid's Corner**.

2. Under **On-Line Coloring Book Endangered Species** you will find a list of pictures of endangered species to color. Select one to print and color. Here is one to try now.

Bald Eagle

The bald eagle is our national symbol. Its eyesight is so good that it can spot a fish from more than a mile away. It is so fast that it can swoop down through the air at 100 miles an hour to catch this tasty meal with its strong claws.

Name_____

 **NetWork: This is for the Birds!**

Overview

Daisy is a yellow and white Lutino cockatiel. Learn more about Daisy and her friends in the cartoon land of Amy and Daisy.

Procedure

With your Web browser access the URL

`http://coastnet.com/dhouston/Amy.html`

Activities

1. Browse through the options at this site. Start by selecting the icon next to the text **Learn more about Daisy and her friends**.

2. What have you learned about birds? Color the bird and the word **bird**.

3. Draw your own bird cartoon.

4. Would you like to have a pet bird? Find out how to choose and take care of it at the site with URL

    `http://www.aloha.net/~granty/`.

Name_____

NetWork: Interactive Fun

Overview

Simon and Schuster supports a Web site for children ages three through eight. Give this interactive site a try.

Procedure

With your Web browser access the URL

`http://www.teachkids.com/`

Activities

1. Select the **counting game** icon. Click on a number and that number of bugs will appear.

    Circle seven bugs.

2. From the home page, select the **coloring game** icon. Choose a picture. Click the color and then the area you wish to color.

3. Try other options at this site.

4. Draw a picture of three bugs and copy the word **bugs**.

b u g s

Name_____

 # NetWork: Breakfast on the Web

Overview

Meet the Kellogg's™ characters; print and color pictures; solve a word find puzzle; read some Snap, Crackle, Pop™ comics; make a greeting card – all in Kellogg's Clubhouse.

Procedure

With your Web browser access the URL

> `http://www.kelloggs.com/club/index.html`

Activities

1. Select the **Lounge** and then **canvas** to find some pictures. Select a picture to color. Click on a color and then on the place to color. Continue until the picture is complete. Go back to the **Lounge** and select **Grapple with the Apple**. Complete the word search puzzle by clicking on the first letter and then on the last letter of each word that you find.

2. Explore other areas of this site.

3. Dictate or write the names of food that you like to eat for breakfast.

_____

_ _

_____

_ _

_____

_ _

_____

Name_____

Chapter Four
NetWork for Young Learners:
Arts, Crafts, Entertainment

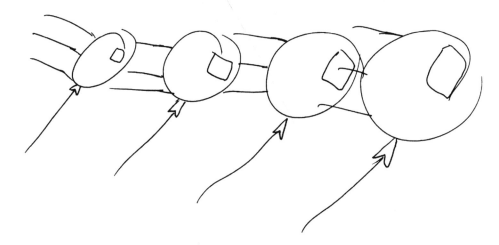

Notes to Teachers and Parents

Art on the Net? You bet. Some activities are interactive and some let you print materials to produce artwork the old fashioned way.

Prerequisites

In order to complete the NetWork in this chapter you will need access to a computer, the Internet network, and World Wide Web browser software.

Objectives

After completion of the NetWork in this chapter, young learners will be able to use the keyboard and mouse to perform basic functions on the computer and the World Wide Web. Participating in interactive art activities as well as following instructions for completing crafts with paint, pencils, coloring crayons, scissors, paper, and other tools will help young children:

- develop small muscle coordination;

- learn to draw pictures of objects;

- learn to draw pictures to represent a story or activity; and

- have fun!

Student Activities

1. Review all materials in this chapter. Test activities. Edit and expand upon worksheets as appropriate for your children.

2. Choose appropriate NetWork worksheets; work through the exercises with the children, maximizing their participation. Read instructions to them or help them read. For writing exercises, children can do the writing or dictate to an adult, the scribe. Talk to them about their discoveries.

3. Extend the exercises and create more activities as appropriate.

References

Chapter Six lists on-line resources for further exploration of the Internet. *Chapter Seven* includes ideas for creating additional NetWork.

◼️📝➤ NetWork: Web-a-Sketch

Overview

Have fun drawing with Web-a-Sketch and enter the contest. Web-a-Sketch rules are consistent with the Etch-a-Sketch™ standards:

- Each line you draw is permanent, there is no "undo."

- There is no lifting up the pen. Entire drawings are done with a single, continuous line.

Procedure

With your Web browser access the URL

http://www.digitalstuff.com/web-a-sketch/

Activities

1. Visit **The Web-A-Sketch Awards** section featuring the site's award-winners and **The Web-a-Sketch Gallery** to view the masterpieces of fellow sketchers.

2. Visit **The Web-a-Sketch Contests** to learn how to enter the contest.

3. To create a Web-a-Sketch, select **Start**. Choose your Web-a-Sketch size and then click the **web-a-sketch** button. Click to create lines, beginning with a click to create your starting point. Click at another spot to create a line between the two points. Continue clicking and each new point will be connected to the last point.

   Click **erase** if you want to start over. If you want to enter your creation into the gallery click the **finished!** button and enter the information requested.

   If you do not want to enter your sketch into the gallery, click **erase**.

4. Create a plan for a Web-a-Sketch entry. In the space below, create a sketch by drawing from dot to dot without lifting your pencil.

Name_____

NetWork: Wish with Wishupons

Overview

Wildheart's™ The Wishupons™ Web site will help make your dreams come true. Meet Quigly™, Sprigs™, Fenton™, Dwirp™, Jewels™, and Murphy™. Download and print coloring pages, dot-to-dots, word scrambles, and puzzles for hours of fun.

Procedure

With your Web browser access the URL

> `http://www.p2000.com/wishupons/index.html`

Activities

1. From the Wishupons home page, select **So come and join Quigly, Sprigs, Fenton, Dwirp, Jewels and Murphy**. Who are these characters?

2. From the home page, select **ACTIVITY CENTER**. Under GAMES select a **Connect the Dots** activity. Print the activity on your printer and complete it with a pencil or coloring crayon. From the home page, select **ACTIVITY CENTER**. Under GAMES select a **Crossword Puzzle** activity. Print on your printer and complete the puzzle with a pencil or coloring crayon.

4. Return to the GAMES area and under the heading COLORING PAGES select a picture, print it on your printer, and color it with coloring crayons.

5. Inside the star, draw something you wish for.

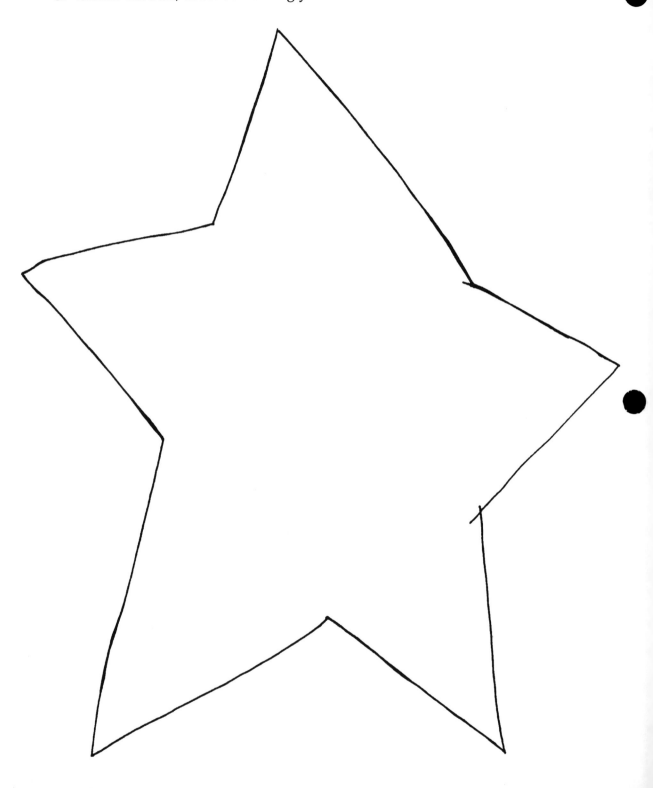

Name_____

NetWork: Enter an Art Contest

Overview

Enter a weekly art contest for kids hosted by The Refrigerator Web site. Finalists are reviewed by visitors to the site. The winning entree is posted on the virtual refrigerator for one week. Hey, you could even print out your entry on a printer and tape it on your refrigerator at home – what a cool idea!

Procedure

With your Web browser access the URL

http://www.seeusa.com/refrigerator.html

It will be helpful to have a printed map of the United States and of the world.

Activities

1. Press **Click Here to See This Week's Winner**.

2. Select **The Competition** to see recent entrees. As you review the pictures, read the names of the entrants, their ages, and the cities and states where they live; read the titles of the pictures. On a map you can see where each entrant lives.

    Type or dictate the end of the sentence `I like this picture because`.

3. Select **Hall of Fame** to review past winners.

4. Choose **Contest Rules** to learn how to enter the contest. Basically, you send in a picture by postal mail. If your entry is one of the top five for the week, it will be in the competition where site visitors vote. If you win, your picture will be featured for a week on the Web site and entered into the Hall of Fame.

5. Draw a picture to put on a real refrigerator.

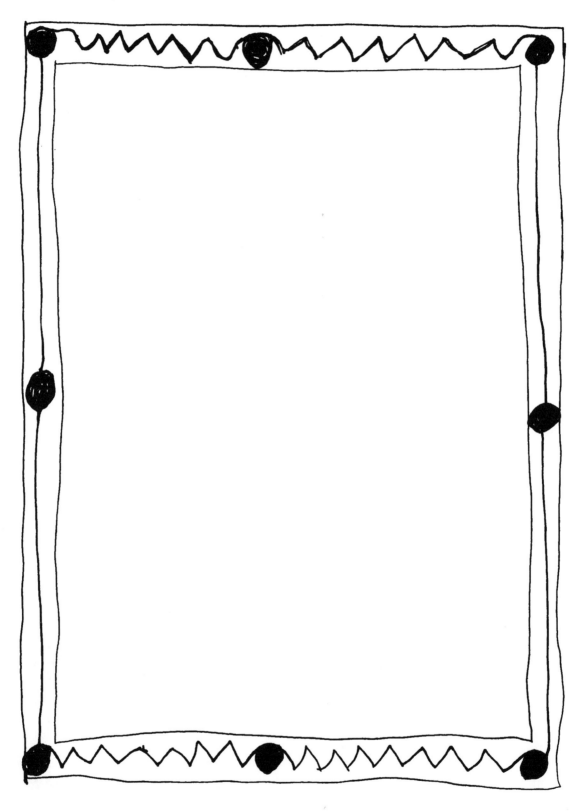

Name_____

NetWork: Color with Carlos

Overview

Carlos' Coloring Book interactive resource is based on James F. Allison's Coloring Book 3.0 for the Macintosh®. You can play with the Internet version of the coloring book or you can download the software to run on a Macintosh computer.

Procedure

With your Web browser access the URL

> **http://www.ravenna.com/coloring/**

Activities

1. Have fun coloring a picture on-line. If you choose **birthday wish** to color, your screen looks like this:

Try coloring the **apple** on-line. Then color the apple below with real coloring crayons.

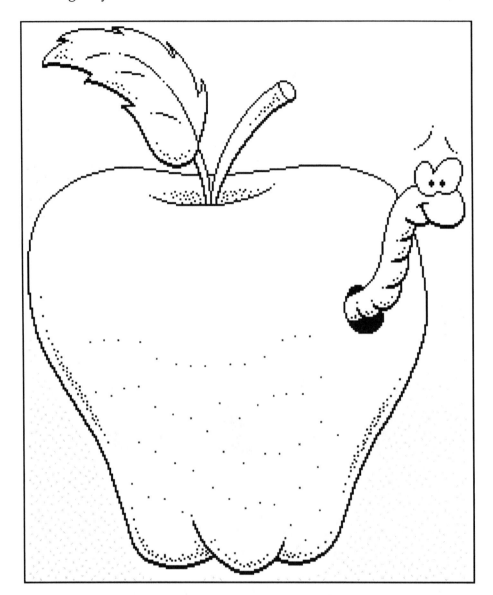

2. To download Coloring Book software, select **Coloring Book 3.0 for Macintosh** from the home page and follow the instructions to download this shareware software to your computer.

    A `Coloring Book` icon will appear on your computer's desktop if you use browser client software on your personal computer. Double click on the icon to run the program. It is pretty easy to follow, but if you need it, `Help General` can be found under the `Parents` menu. Choose a picture and have fun coloring. As you move to new screens with the right arrow you will find an option for creating a story.

Name_____

NetWork: Go On-line with Orbill

Overview

Get absorbed in the interactive Orbill's Coloring Book.

Procedure

With your Web browser access the URL

http://www.delta-air.com/ffl/orb/orb_ocbk.htm

Activities

1. Click on the picture you wish to color. Choose a color and the area to be filled. After you finish a picture, select **CHOOSE ANOTHER PICTURE** to return to the home page and select another picture.

2. From the home page, select **MEET DUSTY AND FRIENDS**. Click on each face pictured on this page to meet the four characters. Write their names.

_____

_ _

_____

_ _

_____

_____

_ _

_____

_____

_ _

_____

Click **RETURN TO HOME PAGE**. Explore other areas of this site.

3. Color a picture of you and your friends.

Name_____

 **NetWork: Color with Kendra**

Overview

Everyone loves to color. Join Kendra in coloring on-line in Kendra's Coloring Book.

Procedure

With your Web browser access the URL

http://www.geocities.com/EnchantedForest/7155/

Activities

1. Choose pictures to color on-line. or click **Print picture** to print out on your printer and color with real coloring crayons.

2. Color your own picture.

Name_____

NetWork: Disney On-line

Overview

Learn about your favorite Disney™ characters on-line, download pictures to color, and participate in interactive activities along the way.

Procedure

With your Web browser access the URL

`http://www.disney.com/`

Activities

1. Select **Walt Disney Home Video**. You'll find some of your favorite Disney movies listed, including

    > Mighty Ducks: The Movie
    > 101 Dalmatians
    > Honey, We Shrunk Ourselves
    > Toy Story
    > The Hunchback of Notre Dame
    > Bambi
    > Aladdin and the King of Thieves
    > James and the Giant Peach
    > Oliver & Company

    Select **101 Dalmations**. You need to help find the puppies. Click **here** to help. Click on animal figures to find clues and try to find the puppies.

2. Select another movie and explore. You'll find information about the characters, coloring pages, and games.

3. Explore other areas at the Disney Web site.

4. Design a Web page for a favorite movie.

Name_____

 NetWork: MCA's Coloring Corner

Overview

Coloring without a color crayon? Yep, it can be done on the Net. Try the site maintained by MCA/Universal Home Video and color some of your favorite characters.

Procedure

With your Web browser access the URL

http://www.mca.com/home/

Activities

1. Select **Coloring Corner** to color pictures of your favorite characters on-line.

2. Choose from among the selections. They include **Babe**, **Balto**, **Casper**, **Timmy the Tooth**, **Littlefoot**, and **Brushbrush**. Click on a color and then the area of the picture to be filled in with that color.

   When finished, select **Back** to return to Coloring Corner and make another selection.

3. After coloring the Timothy the Tooth page at this site, put your own face on this tooth. Name this tooth (your name)-the-Tooth.

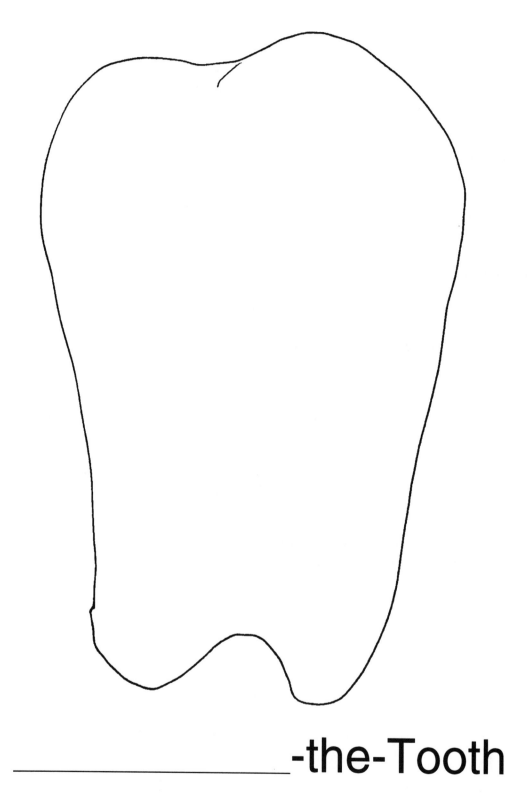

_____-the-Tooth

Name_____

NetWork: Dalmations, Pinocchio, Beauty, Beast, and More!

Overview

It seems that every movie and television show has a Web page. Find pretty pictures and engaging activities to enjoy.

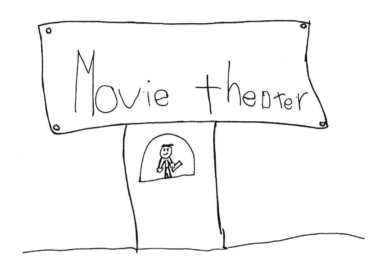

Procedure

With your Web browser access the URLs

The Adventures of Pinocchio
`http://www.pinocchio.com/`

Beauty and the Beast
`http://www.columbia.edu/~zm4/BeautyandBeast/`

Discovery Channel Online
`http://www.discovery.com/`

Disney
`http://www.disney.com/`

Fly Away Home
`http://www.spe.sony.com/Pictures/SonyMovies/movies/`
`    Flyaway/movie.html`

Fox Kids Network
`http://www.foxkids.com/home.htm`

Hercules
`http://www.disney.com/Hercules/`

History Channel's History for Kids
`http://www.historychannel.com/kids/kids.html`

Muppets
`http://www.ncsa.uiuc.edu/VR/BS/Muppets/muppets.html`

Nickelodeon
`http://www.nick.com/auth/tech.html`

Space Jam
`http://www.spacejam.com/`

Star Wars
`http://www.starwars.com/`

Superman
`http://www.superman.com`

Warner Brothers Online™
`http://www.warnerbros.com/`

Activities

1. Explore the sites. Enjoy the pictures, talk about the stories, and create new adventures for your favorite characters.

2. Tell a story about your favorite movie character. Act out the story.

Name_____

 **NetWork: Join the ACEKids**

Overview

You'll have fun with the ACEKids.

Procedure

With your Web browser access the URL

> `http://www.acekids.com/kidshome.html`

Activities

1. Select **Play Our Games** to read stories written by kids. Learn how you can submit your own story.

    Select **Back to AceKids Home Page**.

2. Select **Play Our Games**. Try **Play Connect4**, **Play Hunt the Wumpus**, and other games for kids.

    Select **Back to AceKids Home Page**.

3. Select **Join our Animated Bagel Family**. You'll be able to create an animated bagel with `The Incredible Bagel Maker`. Just select from the choices provided:

    > - Pick A Gender
    > - Pick a Flavor
    > - Choose the Hair
    > - Choose the Eyes
    > - Choose the Shoes

    Click **Make my Bagel** to see your creation.

    Select **Back to AceKids Home Page**.

4. Try other activities at this site. Be sure to try **Other Fun Stuff** and **All the Kid's Links** to find interesting Internet sites to explore.

5. Create a Bagel buddy of your own using coloring crayons. Dress him/her up in some cool clothes and write his/her name.

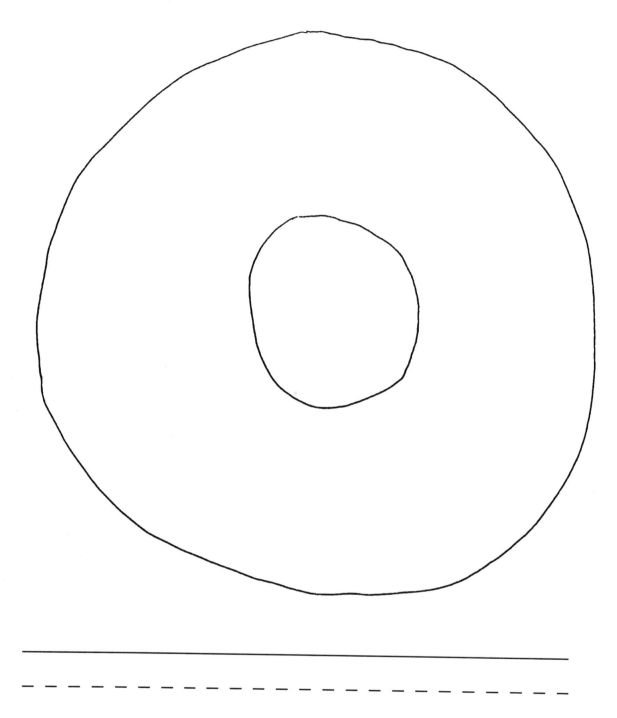

6. Ask your parents if you can decorate a real bagel!

Name_____

 NetWork: Toys, Toys, and More Toys!

Overview

Hot Wheels®, Etch-a-Sketch™, Barbie®, LEGO®, Teenage Mutant Ninja Turtles® on the Net? You bet. Most are commercial sites and have much to sell! However, at a toy site you can also learn about the history of the toy, a newsletter, fun facts, and links to interesting Web sites.

Procedure

With your Web browser access the URLs

Barbie®
http://www.fau.edu/library/barblink.htm

Etch-a-Sketch
http://www.world-of-toys.com/

Hasbro® Toys
http://www2.hasbrotoys.com/hasbro/

Hot Wheels
http://www.hotwheels.com/

Interactive Model Railroad
http://rr-vs.informatik.uni-ulm.de/rr/

LEGO
http://www.lego.com

Matchbox™
http://www.matchboxtoys.com/vehicles/index.html

Teenage Mutant Ninja Turtles
http://www.ninjaturtles.com/

Activities

1. Explore the Web sites for your favorite toys.

2. Draw a picture of a favorite toy and color it.

Name_____

 # NetWork: Crafts for Fun

Overview

Some WWW sites provide great craft ideas. You can print the instructions and templates and then use real pencils, coloring crayons, paste, scissors, and paper to create works of art.

Procedure

To find directions for crafts, with your Web browser access the URLs

Aunt Annie's Craft Page™
`http://www.auntannie.com/`

Children's Activity Page
`http://www.youngartist.com/activity.html`

Crafts for Kids
`http://ucunix.san.uc.edu/~edavis/kids-list/`
`   crafts.html`

Kid's Crafts Bulletin Board
`http://www.wwvisions.com/craftbb/kids.html`

Kids Craft
`http://www.ozemail.com.au/~teasdale/craft.html`

WWW.funroom.com
`http://tac.shopnetmall.com/www.funroom.com/`

Activities

1. What fun activities did you find?

2. What crafts would make good presents for Mothers' Day, Fathers' Day, and birthdays?

3. If you created a craft Web site, describe the projects you would put on it.

Chapter Five
NetWork for Young Learners:
More to Explore

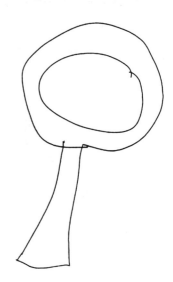

Notes to Teachers and Parents

Many rich resources on the Net can enhance and stimulate learning for young children.

Prerequisites

In order to complete the NetWork in this chapter you will need access to a computer, the Internet network, and World Wide Web browser software.

Objectives

In this chapter children use the World Wide Web to participate in educational and recreational activities. After completion of the NetWork young learners will be able to:

- use the keyboard and mouse to perform basic functions on the computer and the World Wide Web;

- use Internet resources to develop reading, writing, mathematics, science, social studies, and art skills;

- search for Internet resources; and

- have fun on the Internet.

Student Activities

1. Review all materials in this chapter. Test activities. Edit and expand upon worksheets as appropriate for your children.

2. Choose appropriate NetWork worksheets; work through the exercises with the children, maximizing their participation. Read instructions to them or help them read. For writing exercises, children can do the writing or dictate to an adult, the scribe. Talk to them about their discoveries.

3. Help children develop research skills as you search for Internet resources together.

4. Extend the exercises and create more activities as appropriate.

References

Chapter Six lists on-line resources for further exploration of the Internet. *Chapter Seven* includes ideas for creating additional NetWork.

NetWork: Become a Web Explorer

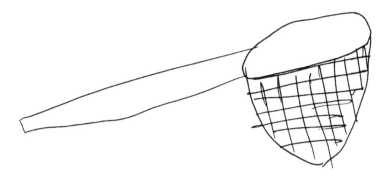

Overview

Sometimes it is not as important to know the right answer as it is to know where to find it. With Little Explorer™ even preschoolers can surf the Web (with a little help and guidance from their favorite adult) using a picture dictionary with links. Each link has been selected to be appropriate, enjoyable, and educational for young learners. Learn and practice reading skills while you use the alphabet to find a topic.

Procedure

With your Web browser access the URL

`http://www.EnchantedLearning.com/Dictionary.html`

Activities

1. Select **Busy Little Brains** to meet Gabyy and Jesse and sample some educational activities. Return to the home page.

2. Click on a letter and you'll see words that start with that letter. Then click on a picture or a word, and you'll link to something cool about that word. For example, click on **B** to view pictures of a baby, bagel, ball, balloons, and more!

   From the home page, your parent or teacher can select **Easy Web Tips to Teach Children** to learn about helping children use the Internet.

4. Match the upper case with the lower case letter.

A	g
B	q
C	h
D	p
E	f
F	o
G	b
H	n
I	z
J	m
K	y
L	a
M	x
N	e
O	w
P	t
Q	v
R	d
S	u
T	k
U	s
V	l
W	j
X	r
Y	i
Z	c

Name_____

 **NetWork: Surf Web Collections**

Overview

There are many collections of children's sites on the Web. Keep a collection of URLs and you'll never be far from a fun activity. Save them as bookmarks with your Web browser. Resources at Web sites are updated regularly, so return often to make new discoveries.

Procedure

With your Web browser access each of the URLs

---

100 Hot Sites for Kids
`http://www.100hot.com/kids/`

aha! Kid's Network
`http://www.aha-kids.com/`

Bennett's Best Web Picks for Kids
`http://www.familysurf.com/`

Berit's Best Sites for Children
`http://db.cochran.com/db_HTML:theopage.db`

BONUS.com™ the Supersite for Kids
`http://www.bonus.com`

Canadian Kids Page
`http://www.onramp.ca/~lowens/107kids.htm`

Children's Pages at WomBatNet
`http://www.batnet.com/wombat/children.html`

Early Childhood Education & Activity Resources
`http://www.intex.net/~dlester/pam/preschool/`
`    preschoolpage.html`

EE-Link: Environmental Education on the Internet
`http://www.nceet.snre.umich.edu/index.html`

Great Links for Young Children
`http://www.intex.net/~dlester/pam/preschoollinks.html`

Kids' Corner
`http://kids.ot.com/`

Kids Place!
`http://www.mdc.net/~hayes/kplace.htm`

Kids' Places
`http://www.reedbooks.com.au/rigby/kids/kidplace.html`

Kids Web
`http://www.npac.syr.edu/textbook/kidsweb/`

Kidsite
`http://www.osu-okmulgee.edu/kidsite.htm#set1`

KidWorld
`http://www.bconnex.net/~kidworld`

Kidz Safe Playground
`http://www.worldvillage.com/kidz/`

Link Pages
`http://www.nauticom.net/www/winnie/kicks.html/`

McGuffie Avenue Gang
`http://www.mcguffie.on.ca/`

Microsoft Kids Network
`http://www.msn.com/`

TnT Cool Stuff for Kids
`http://www.polar7.com/tnt/`

Ultimate Children's Internet Sites
`http://www.vividus.com/ucis.html#preschool`

World Kids Network™
`http://www.worldkids.net/`

Activities

Surf the Web sites and bookmark sites to which you wish to return.

 ## NetWork: Search WWW

Overview

Use search tools to search the Web for things that interest you. Some are organized by topic. Some allow you to use keywords in your search. Once you find a resource of interest to you, click on the name and you will be linked to that site automatically. Below are URLs of some search tools on the Net. Some sites maintain collections of search tools.

```
http://altavista.digital.com/
http://galaxy.einet.net
http://inktomi.berkeley.edu/
http://lycos.cs.cmu.edu/
http://metacrawler.cs.washington.edu/
http://webcrawler.com/
http://www.excite.com/
http://www.four11.com/
http://www.infoseek.com/
http://www.mckinley.com/
http://www.search.com
http://www.yahoo.com/
```

Procedure and Activities

1. Choose a topic that you would like to explore and try several search tools to find Internet sites of interest. Here are some suggestions:

movies	games
toys	coloring
zoo	crafts
Barbie	dogs
trains	soccer

2. Make a list of URLs of Internet resources you find. Better yet, save bookmarks using your WWW browser so that you can easily return to them.

Chapter Six
Find More Stuff: On-line Internet Guides and Directories

Notes to Teachers and Parents

In just about any book store, you can find many useful Internet books. The books get thicker every year and probably include more than you'll ever need (or want) to know about the Internet. You can also find information about the Internet on the Internet itself (what a novel idea!). All of the resources in this chapter can help you develop your own Internet skills as well as create more NetWork for children.

Listed below is a small sample of Internet guides, directories, and other publications for learning more about using the Internet and locating resources on it. The content and quality vary, as with any set of resources on the Net. Some of the options for accessing the resources are listed. Try accessing a few now and refer to this list in the future. You can read them on your screen or print them on your printer.

Guides and Directories

General Internet Information

Argus Clearinghouse, Argus Associates
http://www.clearinghouse.net/

Electronic Frontier Foundation's (Extended) Guide to the Internet, Adam
   Gaffin (formerly *The Big Dummy's Guide to the Internet*, published in
   hard copy by MIT Press as *Everybody's Guide to the Internet*)
ftp://ftp.eff.org, /pub/Net_info/EFF_Net_Guide/
gopher://gopher.eff.org, 1/Net_info/EFF_Net_Guide
http://www.eff.org/papers/eegtti/
Send a request for the *Guide* to netguide@eff.org.

A Gentle Introduction to the Internet, Kristen McQuillin
http://www.lm.com/info/Internet/gentle.html

Global Network Navigator, O'Reilly and Associates
http://nearnet.gnn.com/

Hobbes' Internet Timeline
http://info.isoc.org/guest/zakon/Internet/History/HIT.html

*Information Sources: The Internet and Computer-Mediated
   Communication*, John December
ftp://ftp.rpi.edu/pub/communications/internet-cmc.txt

Internet Guides
http://www.brandonu.ca/~ennsnr/Resources/guides.html

An Internet Primer, Michael Malazdrewicz,
http://www.docker.com/primer.html

Internet Resource Directory for Educators
ftp://tapr.org/pub/ed-telecomputing/

Internet Resources, Heriot-Watt University, Edinburgh, United Kingdom
http://www.hw.ac.uk/libWWW/irn/irn.html

Internet Service Providers by Area Code
http://thelist.com/

Internet TourBus, Patrick Crispen and Bob Rankin
```
http://www.worldvillage.com/tourbus.htm
```
Send electronic mail to `listserv@listserv.aol.com` with a blank
   subject line and **subscribe tourbus *Firstname Lastname*** in the
   body of the message.

Internet Training Archive
```
ftp://nstn.ns.ca/pub/doc
ftp://nstn.ns.ca/pub/mac-stuff
ftp://nstn.ns.ca/pub/pc-stuff
```

InterNIC Directory and Database Service, AT&T Corporation
```
ftp://ftp.sura.net/pub/
http://ds.internic.net/
```

Introduction to the Internet, University of Michigan
```
http://www.sils.umich.edu/~fprefect/inet/
```

Net-Happenings
```
http://www.mid.net/net/
```
Send e-mail to `listserv@lists.internic.net` with a blank subject
   line and **subscribe net-happenings *FirstName Lastname*** in
   the body of the message

Netiquette, Arlene Rinaldi
```
http://www.fau.edu/rinaldi/netiquette.html
ftp://ftp.lib.berkeley.edu/pub/net.training/FAU
   /netiquette.txt
```

The Online World, Odd de Presno
```
http://login.eunet.no/~presno/index.html
```

Roadmap Workshop, Patrick Crispen
```
http://www.ll.mit.edu/Roadmap/WELCOME.html/
```
Send e-mail to `listserv@ua1vm.ua.edu` with a blank subject line and
   get map package F=MAIL in the body of the message

Net Scout Services, InterNIC
```
http://rs.internic.net/scout/
```

The Scout Toolkit, Net Scout Services
```
http://rs.internic.net/scout/toolkit/
```

The Whole Internet Catalog Select, O'Reilly and Associates
```
http://nearnet.gnn.com/wic/
```

Yanoff's Internet Services, Scott Yonoff
```
http://www.spectracom.com/islist/
news:alt.internet.services
ftp://ftp.csd.uwm.edu/pub/inet.services.txt
finger yanoff@alpha2.csd.uwm.edu
```
Send e-mail with no message to `inetlist@aug3.augsburg.edu`

Young Person's Internet Guide
```
http://www.osc.on.ca/kids.html
```

Zen and the Art of the Internet, Brendan P. Kehoe
```
http://ug.cs.dal.ca:3400/online-dir/internet/internet-
    docs/zen.txt
ftp://ftp.internic.net/pub/internet-doc/zen.txt
```

E-mail

Accessing the Internet via E-mail
Send e-mail to `info@wentworth.com` with a blank subject line and **send
    searchmail** in the body of the message
Send e-mail to `listserv@ubvm.cc.buffalo.edu` with a blank subject
    line and **GET Internet by-email nettrain F=MAIL** in the body of the
    message

Electronic Mail Directory Service
```
http://www.four11.com/
```

Inter-Network Mail Guide, Scott Yanoff
```
http://www.nova.edu/Inter-Links/cgi-bin/inmgq.pl
ftp://ftp.csd.uwm.edu/pub/internetwork-mail-guide
```

Distribution/Discussion/Mailing Lists

Biley's List of Listservs and Serials for Librarians
```
gopher://nysernet.org
```

E-mail Discussion Groups
```
http://www.nova.edu/Inter-Links/listserv.html
```

Finding Listserv Discussion Lists
```
gopher://uniwa.uwa.edu.au
gopher://info.umd.edu
```

List of Lists and Publicly Accessible Mailing Lists
```
ftp://sri.com/netinfo/interest-groups.txt
```
Send e-mail to `mail-server@sri.com` with a blank subject line and
    send interest-groups in the body of the message

John December's List of Mailing Lists, John December
```
ftp://ftp.rpi.edu
```

World Wide Web

A Beginner's Guide to HTML
```
http://www.ncsa.uiuc.edu/General/Internet/WWW/HTMLPrimer
    .html
```

A Beginner's Guide to URLs
```
http://www.ncsa.uiuc.edu/demoweb/url-primer.html
```

Entering The World Wide Web, Kevin Hughes
```
http://www.eit.com/web/www.guide/
```

HTML Quick Reference
```
http://kuhttp.cc.ukans.edu/lynx_help/HTML_quick.html
```

HyperText Markup Language (HTML)
```
http://www.w3.org/hypertext/WWW/MarkUp/MarkUp.html
```

Introduction to HTML, Case Western Reserve University
```
http://www.cwru.edu/help/introHTML/toc.html
```

W3 Servers
```
http://www.w3.org/hypertext/DataSources/WWW/Servers.html
```

Web Style Manual, Patrick Lynch
```
http://info.med.yale.edu/caim/StyleManual_Top.HTML
```

WWW & HTML Developer's JumpStation, maintained by SingNet and
    hosted by OneWorld Information Services
```
http://oneworld.wa.com/htmldev/devpage/dev-page.html
```

Gopher/VERONICA/Jughead

Veronica Tutorial
Send e-mail to `info@wentworth.com` with a blank subject line and
    send veronica in the body of the message

Usenet Discussion Groups

Internet Newsgroups
```
http://www.w3.org/hypertext/DataSources/News/Groups/Over
    view.html
```

Usenet News
gopher://gopher.cic.net

Usenet Frequently Asked Questions (FAQs)
gopher://theusc.csd.scarolina.edu

FTP/Archie

Archie Tutorial
Send e-mail to info@wentworth.com with a blank subject line and **send archie** in the body of the message

How to Use Anonymous FTP, P. Deutsch, A. Emtage, Bunyip A. Marine, NASA NAIC
ftp://nic.merit.edu/documents/fyi/fyi24.html

Monster FTP Sites List, University of Illinois
http://hoohoo.ncsa.uiuc.edu/ftp

Chapter Seven
Create More Lessons

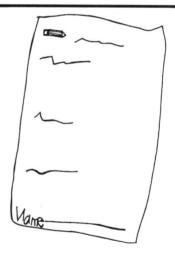

Notes to Teachers and Parents

The World Wide Web is evolving into a viable medium for delivering quality educational and recreational material. But, the Web is not there yet. We're just getting started. To where do we want to get and how will be know when we have arrived?

I would like my son Travis to have Web experiences that are as engaging as the best CD-ROM products, that are appropriate for his developmental level, that build his confidence, that stimulate his interest in learning new things, and that are so flexible that he will want to return to sites again and again.

Web development is progressing at lightning speed to make the Web a single, simple, interactive, integrated working environment. Developments continue to increase the potential for creativity and flexibility in Web applications. The need for integration and interactivity is being addressed by many developers. Web browser developers are reducing the need for "helper" software by building in more capabilities. This trend simplifies the configuration process for users and the development process for Web site developers. The WWW is developing into a better and better medium for the delivery of educational experiences.

Even though we're just beginning to explore the potential of this amazing medium and all is not in place yet, don't get discouraged. You're on the leading edge. Hop in the water and ride the wave to a better future. Rest assured that if you find a resource that is useful today, it will probably be even better the next time you access it. Remember that it takes more than tools to create good materials for children. Parents and teachers need to let Web site developers know their expectations for high quality, appropriate resources for children on the Internet.

Take advantage of the collaborative learning opportunities that the Internet offers you and your children. Assume the role of a facilitator, coach, or guide as you and your children learn side-by-side. Practice alternating the roles of guide and learner as you explore resources together. Make the learning environment child-centered.

When guiding the activities of children, pose questions which address different levels of intellectual behavior. Begin with basic knowledge questions first and progress to open-ended, thought-provoking questions. Cover a variety of the levels of Bloom's taxonomy:

- knowledge,
- comprehension,
- application,
- analysis,
- synthesis, and
- evaluation.

Word questions so that children have a chance to solve problems and to simply explore. Give them opportunities to not only gather information but evaluate the quality of the information and the information service.

Help them gain skills in research, critical thinking, and problem solving. Create activities that maximize participation.

In addition, help children develop and express their attitudes, concerns, and responsibilities – you'll find many opportunities to work in the affective domain while exploring Internet resources. Adjust to different learning styles, skill levels, and levels of enthusiasm about using computers and the Internet.

Consider these concepts as you create new NetWork activities that are tailored to the needs and interests of your children.

Lesson Template

The following template can be used to develop NetWork for your children. Be creative!

Title

Overview

Procedure

Activities

Name_____

Appendix
In Plain English: A Glossary

A B C D e f G H I i K L

A   **address**. Sequence of characters that uniquely identifies an Internet user (e-mail address) or computer.

The American Standards Code for Information Interchange or **ASCII**. A format for representing unformatted text so that it can be read by any computer to which it is transferred.

anonymous FTP. The use of FTP to log on to another computer on which you do not have an account to copy files to your computer, using anonymous as the user name and your e-mail address as the password.

Archie. An Internet search program for locating files that are publicly available from anonymous FTP sites on the Internet.

archive. A collection of electronic files.

ARPANet. The original U. S. government network, the predecessor to the Internet.

B   **baud**. Related to data transfer speed, approximately one bit per second.

binary. A number system that uses only 1's and 0's that is used by computers to store and transfer data.

bit. The smallest unit of information stored on a computer; the basic unit of information in a binary numbering system, 0 or 1.

bits per second or **bps**. A rate of data transfer. For example, a 9600 bps modem is capable of transferring 9600 bits of data per second.

bookmark. A marker that you can keep in your own personal collection using Gopher or WWW so that you can automatically connect to the resource at a later time.

byte. Eight bits of electronic data, the number of bits needed to represent one number or character electronically.

C   **Campus-wide information server** or **CWIS**. An electronic resource developed around the needs of a college or university.

case-sensitive. When the computer application distinguishes between uppercase and lowercase letters.

CERN. Conseil European pour la Recherche Nucleaire, the European Laboratory for Particle Physics.

Chat. On-line, real-time communication where one user types words on a computer and the receiver sees them on his/her screen almost instantaneously (i.e., in real time).

client software. A software application that runs on your behalf to extract a service from a server on the Internet.

command. A direction that you give a computer.

communication software. A program that you run on your personal computer that allows you to call up and communicate with other computers over phone lines.

context-sensitive. When an application can provide information that is relevant to the portion of the program you are using.

cyberspace. Term coined by the author William Gibson to describe the "space" where human minds and computer networks communicate.

D   **data**. Information formatted in a way to make it understood by a computer.

database. Large amounts of information stored in an organized fashion on a computer, like an electronic file cabinet.

dial-up. A connection to a computer made by calling up the computer on a telephone line.

directory. An index to the files and subdirectories that are stored on a computer.

distribution list. A group of people interested in the same topic who subscribe to an e-mail list which is managed by software (e.g., LISTSERV, ListProcessor, or Majordomo).

domain or **domain name**. The name of a computer or group of computers on the Internet.

download. To transfer computer files from another computer to your host or personal computer.

E   **electronic mail**, **e-mail**, or **email**. Electronically transmitted messages.

Eudora™. Electronic mail software with a graphical user interface that runs on a microcomputer.

F   **file**. A collection of information (e.g., text, graphic, software program) stored under one name on a computer.

file transfer protocol or **FTP**. An Internet tool that allows you to copy files from one computer to another on the Internet.

finger. A program that displays information about a user's login file.

flame. Excessive outrage, often virulent and personally insulting, expressed to someone on-line.

freenet. An organization that provides free Internet access to people in a community, often accessible over the Internet.

freeware. Software that you are free to use without charge.

frequently asked questions or **FAQ**. A document posted to answer questions of new users of a service, e.g. à Usenet newsgroup.

G   **gateway**. A computer system that transfers data between normally incompatible networks.

gigabyte. 2^{10} or 1024 megabytes, or 1,073,741,824 bytes.

Gopher. A menu-driven system for connecting to a variety of Internet resources.

Gopherspace. All of the information on the Internet that is available through Gopher.

graphics. Images and pictures.

H   **home page**. The first page you encounter when you access a WWW site.

host. A computer that is connected to the Internet and can provide access to Internet tools such as Gophers, Telnet, and FTP.

hyperlink. Electronic link between WWW pages and files.

hypertext. The capability to link a word or phrase in one document to another related document.

HyperText Markup Language or **HTML**. A markup language used for writing pages for the World Wide Web.

HyperText Transfer Protocol or **HTTP**. The protocol for transferring WWW pages over the Internet.

I   **icon**. A pictorial representation.

Integrated Services Digital Network or **ISDN**. A high-speed, digital telephone service.

Internet. The world-wide collection of networks that are connected and which use a common protocol suite so that they can function as one large network.

Internet Protocol or **IP**. One of the protocols that defines the Internet; IP allows data to traverse multiple networks on its way to its final destination.

Internet service provider. An organization that provides access to the Internet.

J   **Jughead**. An Internet search tool that can scan a Gopher site for material related to a keyword.

K   **keyword**. Word or part of word used to search on-line menus, documents, or databases for entries of interest.

kilobyte or **K**. 2^{10} or 1024 bytes.

L   **link**. A connection between two computers or files.

ListProcessor™. Like LISTSERV, a set of programs that manages electronic discussion lists.

LISTSERV. A set of programs that manages electronic discussion lists.

log on. The procedure to sign on a host computer in order to use it.

login name. The name you use when you log on a host computer to begin a session. Also called ID, account name, or user name.

logout. When you quit using (or, log off) a computer.

lurking. Reading others' messages but never posting your own messages to a discussion list or Usenet newsgroup.

Lynx™. A text-based browser that can be used to access the World Wide Web.

M   **mailbox**. An electronic storage area for your e-mail messages.

Majordomo. Like LISTSERV, a set of programs that manages electronic discussion lists.

megabyte or **M**. 2^{10} or 1024 kilobytes, or 1,048,576 bytes.

menu. Options listed on the screen that lead to documents or other menus.

message. One piece of electronic mail or a single posting in a newsgroup.

Microsoft Internet Explorer®. Microsoft's graphical browser that can be used to access the World Wide Web.

modem. The device that allows a computer to transmit information over a phone line.

MOO. MUD Object-Oriented, a type of Multi-User Dungeon that has a graphical user interface.

MUD. Multiple-User Dungeon, software developed to support on-line real-time role-playing games on the Internet.

N   **NCSA Mosaic™**. A graphical World Wide Web browser developed by the National Center for Supercomputing Applications (NCSA) at the University of Illinois in Urbana-Champaign.

Net. Short for Internet.

netiquette. Generally accepted etiquette on the Internet.

Netscape Navigator™. A graphical browser that can be used to access the World Wide Web.

network. A group of computers connected together.

Network News Transfer Protocol or **NNTP**. The protocol used by local servers that provide access to Usenet newsgroups. NNTP allows Usenet news messages to be transferred between computers on the Internet.

newsgroup. A Usenet bulletin board discussion about a specific topic.

newsreader software. Software that allows you to read Usenet newsgroups.

NSFNET. Internet network created by the National Science Foundation.

O   **on-line**. When you are logged onto a computer.

operating system. Basic software that runs a computer (e.g., Windows, UNIX, VMS, or Macintosh™ System 7).

P   **page**. A document on the WWW.

password. A secret code that gives you access to a system, but keeps your computer area private.

PINE™. An e-mail program developed at the University of Washington.

port. A number that identifies an input or output channel of a computer.

posting. The act of sending a message to a discussion list, Usenet newsgroup or bulletin board.

Point-to-Point Protocol or **PPP**. Protocol that allows a computer to use Internet protocols over standard telephone lines using a high-speed modem.

prompt. A symbol (e.g., >, % : or $) indicating the computer is waiting for your input. For example, `ftp>` is an ftp prompt.

protocol. A set of rules or procedures.

public domain. Files and programs that you are free to use without charge.

R **real time**. An almost immediate response (e.g., with Chat you communicate in real time; with electronic mail you do not).

remote computer. A computer that your personal computer connects to via phone lines or a direct Internet connection.

S **search engine**. Software that allows you to search for resources on the Internet.

server. A computer that provides services on the Internet, such as electronic mail, Gopher, or WWW.

server software. Software running on a server computer.

shareware. Computer software that people can try out without charge but are asked to pay for if they continue using it.

shell. On a Unix computer, software that accepts and processes commands from the user. For example, at a host system prompt you can type a command like **cd** to indicate that you wish to change to another directory.

Serial Line Internet Protocol or **SLIP**. A protocol that allows a computer to use Internet protocols over standard telephone lines using a high-speed modem.

smiley. A picture of a smiling face on its side, e.g., :-).

snail mail. Mail handled by the post office.

software application. A program that runs on a computer and performs a useful function (e.g., e-mail software).

software program. Instructions to a computer that tell it what to do in order to provide the functionality people want (e.g., word processing, electronic mail).

subscribe. To join a distribution list or Usenet newsgroup.

system administrator. Someone who operates and maintains a computer system.

supercomputer. A large, expensive computer that operates much faster than a typical desktop computer and is often used for scientific applications and research.

surfing. Leisurely browsing the Internet.

T

Telnet. A terminal emulation protocol that allows you to log on to another computer on the Internet. NCSA Telnet was developed at the National Center for Supercomputing Applications (NCSA) at the University of Illinois in Urbana-Champaign.

terabyte. 2^{10} or 1024 gigabytes or 1,099,511,627,776 bytes.

terminal. Equipment used to access a host computer.

text. Words or other sequences of letters and numbers.

thread. A discussion on a specific topic in a newsgroup on distribution list.

Transmission Control Protocol/Internet Protocol or **TCP/IP**. A system of rules that allows computers to communicate over the Internet.

U

Uniform Resource Locator or **URL**. An address for a site on the Internet expressed in a standard format.

Unix. The operating system most often used on Internet host computers.

unsubscribe. To remove your name from the membership list of a distribution list or Usenet newsgroup.

upload. Sending a file from your computer to another computer.

Usenet. Bulletin board systems that host newsgroup forums, each of which provides discussion on a particular topic.

user. Anyone using a computer.

V **VERONICA**. A tool that allows you to search all Gopher sites for menu items of interest.

virtual. Being in essence or effect but not in fact.

W **Web browser**. Client software that allows you to navigate through the WWW and search for, read, and download documents, graphics, sound, and video.

Wide Area Information Server or **WAIS**. Unix-based software used to search archives on the Internet.

World Wide Web, W3, WWW, or **Web**. A system for organizing information on the Internet using hypertext links.

Index

100 Hot Sites for Kids 159
101 Dalmatians 143
ACEKids 149
adaptive technology xvii, 8
address xv, 7, 10, 16, 173
adoption 8, 11
adoptive parents 8
airplanes 81, 82
Aladdin and the King of Thieves 143
Alex's Scribbles 33
Alice in Internetland 39
Alice's Adventures in Wonderland.
    39
alphabet 37, 38, 43, 54, 75, 83, 108,
    157, 158
Amy and Daisy 123

animals 37, 56, 74, 75, 95, 96, 97, 107,
    108, 119, 121
aquarium 80, 107
Archie 168, 173
archive 14, 173
ARPANet 3, 173
Arthur xvi, 23, 27
arts 129
ASCII 173
Aunt Annie's Craft Page 153
Awesome Cyber Cards 49
Babe 145
babies 8
Balto 145
Bambi 143
Barbie 151
Barney 23

baud 174
Beantime Stories 85
Bennett's Best Web Picks for Kids 159
Berit's Best Sites for Children 58, 159
Bess, the Internet Retriever 11, 18
Billy Bear 101, 102
binary 174
birds 123
bit 174
bits per second (bps) 174
Bloom's Taxonomy xvi
BONUS.com 159
bookmark 174
BookWire Electronic Children's
    Books 75
BoomerWolf 108
Brave and Bold Squirrel 43
browser software xvii, 9, 10, 170
Brushbrush 145
Build-A-Card 49
Build-a-Monster 99
butterflies 91
Buzzy Bee 35
byte 174
campus-wide information server
    (CWIS) 13, 174
Canadian Kids Page 159
Candlelight Stories 45
Captain Quest 93
Carlos' Coloring Book 137
case-sensitive xix, 174
Casper 106, 145
CERN 9, 174
Chat 174
Chateau Meddybemps 85
child safety 17, 55
child safety guidelines 17
Children's Activity Page 153
Children's Pages at WomBatNet 159
Children's Storybooks Online 35
Children's Zoo Pages 107
Childrens' Television Workshop 112
Classics for Young People 75
Classroom Connect 11
Clearinghouse on Elementary and
    Early Childhood Education 11

client software 9, 174
Closing the Gap 11
Coco and Loco Cat Page 119
coloring 21, 23, 31, 35, 36, 55, 56, 57,
    58, 79, 81, 82, 87, 91, 95, 103, 105,
    109, 110, 115, 122, 126, 127, 133,
    137, 138, 139, 141, 143, 145, 146
command xviii, 174
communication software 174
Concertina 75
Connect Four 149
connect-the-dots 41, 95, 103, 105, 133
Connect4 149
context-sensitive 174
counting 78, 93, 94, 112, 125
crafts 129, 153
Crafts for Kids 153
Crayola 115
crossword puzzle 133
Cub Den 108
Curious George 65
CWIS 174
CyberMom 11
cyberspace 174
data 14, 174, 175
database 175
dial-up 175
dinosaurs 103
directory 10, 175
disabled children xvii
Discovery Channel Online 147
Disney 143
distribution list 4, 7, 166, 175
    basics 7
    help 8
    ListProc 7
    LISTSERV 7
    lurk 7
    Majordomo 7
    post 7
    reply 7
    subscribe 7, 180
    unsubscribe 8, 180
domain 175
dot-to-dot 41, 95, 103, 105, 133
download 175

Dr. Seuss 19, 41, 42
Early Childhood Education &
    Activity Resources 11, 159
easi 8
Educational Software Institute 11
EE-Link 159
Electric Postcard 49
electronic mail 4, 5, 10, 166, 175
Endangered Species 121
entertainment 129
Environmental Education on the
    Internet 159
Etch-a-Sketch 131, 151
Eudora 5, 175
Evil Mathematician 93
FACES of Adoption 11
Family Planet 11
Family Surfboard 108
Family.com 12
file 3, 4, 9, 10, 13, 14, 16, 175
file transfer protocol (FTP) 4, 9, 10,
    14, 168, 173, 175
finger 175
Fish Information Service 80
flame 175
Florida Aquarium 80
Fly Away Home 147
Fox Kids Network 148
freenet 175
freeware 175
frequently asked questions (FAQ)
    175
Froggy Page 108
gateway 176
geography 95, 135
gifted kids 8
gigabyte 176
Global SchoolNet 12
Gopher 4, 9, 10, 13, 167, 176
Gopherspace 176
government 73
Grandad's Animal Alphabet Book 75,
    108
graphics 176
Hello Kitty 71
Hercules 148

Herp Pictures 108
Hip-O 93
home page 9, 176
home schooling 11
Honey, We Shrunk Ourselves 143
host 176
Hot Wheels 151
HotList of K-12 Internet School Sites
    12
Hunchback of Notre Dame 143
hyperlink 9, 176
hypertext 9, 176
HyperText Markup Language
    (HTML) 167, 176
HyperText Transfer Protocol (HTTP)
    10, 176
icon 176
Instructional Television 12
Interactive Model Railroad 151
International Kids' Space 63
Internet xi, 1, 3, 176
    basics 3
    guides 164
    introduction 1
    references 2
    student activities 2
Internet Greeting Cards 49
Internet Protocol (IP) 3, 176
Internet service provider xvii, 4, 5,
    10, 164, 176
ISDN 176
James and the Giant Peach 143
Jay Jay 81
Jughead 167, 177
Jump Start Grade School 105
Jump Start Kids 103
Katie's Quest 21
Kellogg's Clubhouse 127
Kendra's Coloring Book 141
keyword 15, 161, 177
Kid's Corner 91, 121
Kid's Crafts Bulletin Board 153
KidPub 69
Kids Craft 153
Kids Place! 160
Kids Web 160

Kids' Corner 160
Kids' Net 59
Kids' Places 160
Kidsite 160
KidSource OnLine 12
KIDSPHERE 8
KidsXone 93
KidWorld 160
Kidz Safe Playground 160
kilobyte 177
Knowledge Adventure 103, 105
Knoxville Zoo 107
Kody's Beary Scary Story 53
"Kody's Home" Page 53
Lamb Chops Play-Along 23, 24
language arts 19
Learning Train 12
LEGO 151
link xiii, 9, 10, 177, 181
Link Pages 160
list manager software 7, 177
List Server Page 15
ListProcessor 7, 177
LISTSERV 7, 177
Liszt 15
Little Explorer 157
Littlefoot 145
Littlest Knight Coloring Book 36
log on 4, 13, 177, 180
login name 177
logout 177
lurking 7, 177
Lynx 177
magic squares, 67
mailbox 177
Majordomo 7, 177
Matchbox 151
mathematics 77
maze 41, 61, 97
MCA/Universal Home Video 145
McGuffie Avenue Gang 51, 160
megabyte 177
menu 13, 177
message 177
Metro Washington Park Zoo 107
Micke Grove Zoo 107

Microsoft Internet Explorer 177
Microsoft Kids Network 160
Mighty Ducks 143
missing children 11, 12
Mister Rogers' Neighborhood 24
modem xvii, 177
Monterey Bay Aquarium 80
MOO 178
MooTown 37
Mother Goose 29, 75
Mother Goose Gazette 29
movies 143, 145, 147, 148
Mr. Edible Starchy Tuber Head 113
Mr. Flibby 83
Mr. Potatohead 113, 114
Mr. Rogers' Neighborhood 23, 31
MUD 178
Muppets 148
My Hero 47
NASA Web site 89
National Center for Missing and
    Exploited Children 12
NCSA Mosaic 178
Net xix, 3, 178
Net Full of Animals 108
Net Nanny 18
netiquette 178
Netscape 178
network 3, 178
Network News Transfer Protocol
    (NNTP) 178
newsreader software 14, 178
Nickelodeon 148
Northwest Trek Animal Park 107
NSFNET 3, 178
objectives
    arts 130
    crafts 130
    entertainment 130
    exploration 156
    language arts 20
    mathematics 78
    parents and teachers 2
    science 78
    social studies 20
off-line xii

Oliver & Company 143
on-line xii, 178
Online Children's Stories 75
operating system 178
Orbill's Coloring Book 139
Our Penguin Fact Book 108
page 9, 178
Parent Soup 12
parenting 8, 11, 12
ParentsPlace.com 12
password 178
PBS 12, 24, 27, 31
Phoenix Zoo 107
PINE 5, 178
Platypus Family Playroom 61
port 178
post 7, 8, 14, 178
PPP 179
prompt 179
protocol 10, 179
public domain 179
Publicly Accessible Mailing Lists 15
Rainbow Land 97
reading xii, 19, 20, 25, 26, 27, 33, 36,
    39, 45, 47, 53, 59, 61, 69, 85, 94, 97,
    111, 119, 149
real time 174, 179
recycling 109, 110
Recycling Coloring Book 109
Refrigerator Web site 135
remote computer 9, 179
Resources for Families of Missing
    Children 12
safety 17, 55
Scholastic Place 87
science 77
scrambled words 67
search engine 15, 179
Sedgwick County Zoo 107
Select-a-Dog 108
server 9, 13, 179
server software 179
Sesame Street 23, 111
Seussville 41
shareware 179
shell 179

Shining Time Station 23
Silly Billys World 75
SLIP 179
smiley 179
snail mail 5, 179
social studies 19, 20
software application 179
software program xiii, 180
space 89
Space Jam 148
special needs kids 8
Star Wars 148
stay-at-home parenting 8
Storybooks Online 35
Storytime 24
subscribe 7, 8, 180
Summer Fun 12
supercomputer 3, 180
Superman 148
surfing 15, 180
SurfWatch 18
system administrator 180
TCP/IP 180
Teachers Helping Teachers 12
Technology and Information
    Educational Services 12
Teenage Mutant Ninja Turtles 151
television 147
Telnet 4, 9, 10, 13, 180
terabyte 180
terminal 180
text 180
The Adventures of Hip-O 93
The Adventures of Pinocchio 147
The Hunchback of Notre Dame 143
The List Server Page 15
The Magic School Bus 23, 87
Theodore Tugboat 57
Theodore Tugboat Online Activity
    Centre 57
thread 180
Tic Tac Toe 117
Timmy the Tooth 145
TnT Cool Stuff for Kids 160
Tots TV 23, 24
Toy Story 143

Trek Kids 107

U.S. Department of Education 12

Ultimate Children's Internet Sites 160

Uniform Resource Locator (URL) 10,
    16, 180

United States Geological Survey 91

Unix 180

unsubscribe 7, 8, 180

upload 180

Usenet Newsgroups 10, 14, 167, 178,
    180

user 4, 180

USGS Biological Resources 91, 121

USGS Learning Web 91, 121

VERONICA 167, 181

virtual 181

Wacky Web Tales 29

WAIS 181

Wangaratta Primary School 95

Warner Brothers Online 148

Web browser 9, 181

Web-a-Sketch 131, 132

Web66 12

Webster the Spider 25

WebTime Stories 25

Whale Times Kid's Page 108

White House 73

Wildheart 133

Wishupons 133

Wizard of Oz 75

word find puzzle 127

World Kids Network 160

World Wide Web (WWW, W3) 4, 9,
    10, 13, 167, 181
    search engine 15, 161, 179

WorldVillage Kidz 101

writing xii, 20, 22, 26, 27, 28, 34, 36,
    52, 56, 59, 62, 67, 69, 70, 84, 95, 96,
    127, 150

writing conventions xviii

WWW.funroom.com 153

WWW4teachers 12

Wyland Kid's Web 79

Yanoff's Internet Services List 15

zoo 107, 108

Zoo in the Wild 108

ZooNet 107

Permissions/Trademarks/Copyrights

America Online is a registered service mark of America Online, Inc.

Arthur is a trademark of Marc Brown.

Aunt Annie's Craft Page is a trademark of Dorothy LaFara.

Awesome Cyber Cards is a trademark of marlo.com.

Barbie and Hot Wheels are registered trademarks of Mattel, Inc.

Barney is a registered trademark of The Lyons Group.

Hasbro is a registered trademark of Lucasfilm Ltd.

Berit's Best Sites for Kids © Cochran Interactive 1995-1997; all rights reserved. Screen images reproduced with permission.

Bess, the Internet Retriever is a trademark of N2H2, Incorporated.

Big Bag, Sesame Street, Sesame Street Parents, and Children's Television Workshop are trademarks of Children's Television Workshop.

BONUS.com is a trademark of The Bonus Network Corporation.

BoomerWolf is a trademark of the New England Wolf Educational Foundation. Buzzy Bee, and other stories on Children's Storybooks Online are trademarked by their authors.

Candlelight Stories is a trademark of Alexander Cima.

Carlos Coloring Book WWW pages reproduced with permission of Carlos A. Pero.

Chateau Meddybemps is a trademark of Jerry Jindrich.

Coloring Book 3.0 for the Macintosh is a registered trademark of James F. Allison.

Courier is a registered trademark of Smith Corona.

CyberMom and the CyberMom logo are service marks of CyberMom Publications.

CyberPatrol is a registered trademark of Microsystems Software.

Disney is a trademark of the Walt Disney Company.

Dr. Seuss is a trademark of Dr. Seuss Enterprises, L.P.

Educational activities were developed by Outreach Extensions.

Etch-a-Sketch is a trademark of the Ohio Art Company.

Eudora is a registered trademark of the University of Illinois Board of Trustees, licensed to QUALCOMM Incorporated.

Family Planet is a service of Starwave Corporation.

Family Surfboard is a trademark of Steve and Ruth Bennett.

GREEN VALLEY Recycling Coloring Book screen images were provided by Green Valley Recycling, California.

Internet Gopher is a trademark of the University of Minnesota.

Jay Jay the Jet Plane was created by David and Deborah Michel and is a trademark of Jay Jay Enterprises. Screen images reproduced with permission.

Kellogg's and Snap! Crackle! Pop! are trademarks of Kellogg Company.

KidSource OnLine is a trademark of KidSource OnLine, Inc.

Kino, Kino's Storytime, and Storytime are trademarks of Community Television of Southern California.

Knowledge Adventure is a trademark of Knowledge Adventure, Inc.

NOTES

NOTES

NOTES

NOTES

NOTES

NOTES

NOTES

NOTES

NOTES

NOTES

NOTES

NOTES

NOTES

NOTES